LETTERS
FROM ZAIRE
A PEACE CORPS
LIFE IN AFRICA

D1572490

JOHN S. JOCHUM

WINEPRESS **WP** PUBLISHING

ISBN 1-57921-753-2
Library of Congress Catalog Card Number: 2004093847

Dedication

To Jesus Christ
My Creator, Savior, Sustainer.

To my parents
Joseph and Mary Jochum
My providers and mentors.

To the people of Bandundu Province, Zaire, Africa
Who treated me with both kindness and a generosity
beyond their means.

The Jochum family, 1978

John, Jim, Paul, Ann, Jerry, Matt (held), Mom, Joe, Dad, Tom
Rose, Sue, Bob

"Lord, when did we see You hungry and feed You,
Or thirsty and give You drink?
When did we see You a stranger and take You in,
Or naked and clothe You?
Or when did we see You sick, or in prison,
And come to You?"

And the King will answer and say to them,
"Assuredly, I say to you,
Inasmuch as you did it
To one of the least
Of these My brethren,
You did it to Me."

Matthew 25:37b–40

Give a man a fish, and he'll eat for a day.
Teach a man to fish, and he'll eat for a lifetime.

Chinese proverb

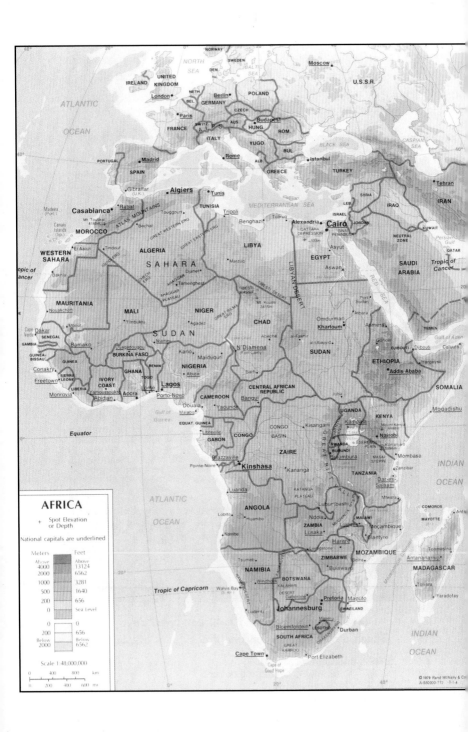

NORWAY
SWEDEN
NORTH SEA
BALTIC SEA
DEN
Moscow
IRELAND
UNITED KINGDOM
NETH
Berlin
POLAND
U.S.S.R.
London
GERMANY
CZECH
Paris
Budapest
FRANCE
SWITZ.
A L P S
AUS
HUNG
ROM.
ITALY
YUGO
BUL.
BLACK SEA
CASPIAN SEA
PORTUGAL
Madrid
Rome
Istanbul
TURKEY
SPAIN
GREECE
ALB
Tehran
Gibraltar (U.K.)
Algiers
Tunis
SYRIA
IRAQ
IRAN
Casablanca
Rabat
TUNISIA
LEB
Madeira (Port.)
ATLAS MOUNTAINS
Tripoli
MEDITERRANEAN SEA
ISRAEL
JORDAN
KUWAIT
Mt Toubkal 4165m
Touggourt
Benghazi
Tobruq
Alexandria
Cairo
Neutral Zone
Persian Gulf
MOROCCO
Bechar
SINAI PENINSULA
QATAR
Canary Islands (Sp.)
GREAT WESTERN ERG
GREAT EASTERN ERG
QATTARA DEPRESSION
-133m
WESTERN SAHARA
El Aaiun
Tindouf
ALGERIA
LIBYA
EGYPT
SAUDI ARABIA
Tropic of Cancer
Tropic of Cancer
Dakhla
S A H A R A
Djanet
Marzuq
Aswan
AHAGGAR PLATEAU
Asyut
MAURITANIA
Nouakchott
MALI
Tamenghest
NIGER
CHAD
TIBESTI MASSIF
Mt Koussi 3415m
LIBYAN DESERT
Omdurman
Port Sudan
Atbara
Asmera
YEMEN
Timbuktu
Agadez
Abeche
al-Fashir
Khartoum
Gulf of Aden
Cape Verde
Dakar
SENEGAL
BILMA ERG
Gonder
Djibouti
DJIBOUTI
Caluula
GAMBIA
Bamako
Niamey
Kano
N'Djamena (Fort-Lamy)
SUDAN
al-Ubayyid
Hargeysa
GUINEA-BISSAU
Ouagadougou
BURKINA FASO
Maiduguri
ETHIOPIA
Conakry
GUINEA
BENIN
NIGERIA
Sarh
Addis Ababa
SIERRA LEONE
GHANA
TOGO
Abuja
CENTRAL AFRICAN REPUBLIC
SOMALIA
Freetown
IVORY COAST
Lome
Lagos
Juba
Monrovia
LIBERIA
Yamoussoukro
Accra
Porto-Novo
CAMEROON
Bangui
Mogadishu
Abidjan
Douala
Yaounde
UGANDA
Gulf of Guinea
Malabo
EQUAT. GUINEA
Kisangani
Kampala
KENYA
Mount Kenya
Equator
Libreville
CONGO
GABON
CONGO BASIN
ZAIRE
RWANDA
BURUNDI
Nairobi
Kilimanjaro
Mombasa
INDIAN OCEAN
Brazzaville
Bujumbura
SERENGETI PLAIN
MASAI STEPPE
Zanzibar
Pointe-Noire
Kinshasa
Kananga
TANZANIA
Dar es Salaam
Luanda
KATANGA PLATEAU
Mtwara
ATLANTIC OCEAN
COMOROS
MAYOTTE
AFRICA
Lobito
ANGOLA
Lubumbashi
Ndola
MALAWI
Mocambique
+ Spot Elevation or Depth
Huambo
ZAMBIA
Toamasina
National capitals are underlined
Namibe
Lusaka
Harare
MOZAMBIQUE
Antananarivo
MADAGASCAR
Meters Feet
Above 4000 / Above 13124
Tsumeb
ZIMBABWE
Buluwayo
Beira
Toliara
2000 / 6562
Bulawayo
1000 / 3281
NAMIBIA
BOTSWANA
Faradofay
500 / 1640
200 / 656
KALAHARI DESERT
Windhoek
0 / Sea Level
Tropic of Capricorn
Walvis Bay
Gaborone
Pretoria
Maputo
0 / 0
Maseru
200 / 656
Luderitz
Johannesburg
SWAZILAND
Below 2000 / Below 6562
Bloemfontein
LESOTHO
Durban
INDIAN OCEAN
Scale 1:48,000,000
SOUTH AFRICA
GREAT KARROO
0   400   800 km
Cape Town
Port Elizabeth
0   200   400   600 mi
Cape of Good Hope
© 1979 Rand McNally & Co.
A-580000-772

Table of Contents

Foreword

John Jochum and I met at a soccer game, and, from the first moment, I knew he was cut from some very special cloth. He gave me the immediate impression that there was much more to him than what met the eye, and, as time has gone on, he has proven that my intuition was right. Soon after the game, John stopped by my university office and handed me a manuscript of his adventures in the Peace Corps. Being a little busy, I read bits and pieces of it but had to let it rest prominently on my desk as the semester dragged to an end. John called after the semester ended and asked what I thought of it. I told him that I was going to finish it soon. It was Christmas Eve, and, having graded the last paper, finished the last correspondence, and sent my staff home early, I picked his manuscript up and began to read. I think in hindsight that the content of the book, combined with the absolute peacefulness of an empty office on Christmas Eve, had a synergistic effect. I found I couldn't put it down.

The Peace Corps has provided many thousands of people over the last five decades with adventure, life-changing experiences, and, above all, a deep appreciation for what they have and a deeper perspective on life. Being a Peace Corps volunteer is arguably an exhilarating experience as many volunteers have stated in books, articles, plays, public lectures, and in the way they have taken what they have learned and lived their lives. Having the opportunity to learn other languages, customs, and traditions, as well as to master practical skills such as aquaculture farming and agriculture techniques provides an intense learning and growing experience for Peace Corps volunteers. However, as John knows, it is what others teach us that will make the biggest difference. It is a wonderful experience when a villager teaches the unwritten rules and expectations of village life that, at first glance, seem illogical or even bizarre only to have an epiphany where things become crystal clear and meaningful. That surprise and exhilaration is true learning. In one sense that's what this book is all about, gaining a perspective on life by focusing outward on others so we can sharpen our introspective growth.

In this collection of letters, John takes us through his personal transformation. We are privy to his inner thinking on current events, the day-to-day challenges in serving others, his relationship with fellow volunteers, the stops and starts of development programs, and his strong connection to his family thousands of miles away. We see a young man coming of age wanting to help other people who are on the brink of civil war.

Throughout the letters, John also shows us his adventurous and inquisitive side. He isn't all about program development, and manages to live and experience the home country in ways tourists and visitors rarely observe, and much less actively seek. There are some youthful, joyful experiences that let us know he isn't seeking sainthood!

When John found his Peace Corps letters neatly stored with loving care in a box in a bedroom drawer of his parents' house, it may have at first seemed as though he had found a personal treasure. However, the lessons John learned and wrote about provide a personal touch to many of the lessons we all eventually need to experience. So after John's sharing these letters with us, we can't help but be introspective about our own lives and how we have come to think about the world, other people, and how we conduct our lives.

A cultural anthropologist, an historian, or a political scientist would find this book a fascinating read as it touches on each of these, often abstract disciplines, from concrete field experiences. However, this book is not meant for that type of audience, but for you, a person who is seeking some deeper meaning in learning about the lives and events of other people. For, in the end, one thing is clear. As you read this book you'll see a young man who has taken a trip of sorts, not a journey to Africa with some considerable physical hardship, but a journey that many people accomplish much later in life. It isn't a long journey; in fact, the journey is rather short, but it can be tough. John has made the journey from his head to his heart. That's the real gift of this book, and that's the real adventure found in these pages.

Dr. Brian Polkinghorn
Associate Professor of Conflict Resolution
Executive Director
Center for Conflict Resolution
Salisbury University, Salisbury, Maryland

Preface

Letters from Zaire—A Peace Corps Life in Africa, is a compilation of personal letters written between 1975 and 1979 to the members of my family in Maryland. Each letter was transcribed in its entirety with a few editorial changes and some deletions of personal items. Several letters were lost in the mail between Africa and the USA, so there are a couple of lapses in the story.

Some references are made to the drinking of alcoholic beverages, for it is a part of the African culture. Being aware of the social, physical, and spiritual hardships alcohol has wrought on the lives of so many, I hope to offend no one for having included these items in the book.

The book cover and each chapter header have a scanned letter as a background. A Zairian street artist in Kinshasa created the artwork on these pages of airmail stationery. The photos on the front cover, page 5, and the first page of each chapter are as follows:

Acknowledgements

The author wishes to express his thanks to:

- his wife, Karen, for living with a dreamer,
- his son, Stephen, for transcribing the manuscript faithfully,
- his sister-in-law, Elizabeth, for proofreading tirelessly,
- and his family, for their unending love and support.

Introduction

In 1961, President John F. Kennedy instituted the United States Peace Corps. Though I was only a young boy of seven, I remember being intrigued by the thought of traveling to a foreign country to help poor people in need. Through the sixties, the television spots advertising "The toughest job you'll ever love" kept the thought fresh. Early in my senior year at the University of Maryland I decided to apply to see if I could be of any service.

In 1975, the U.S. Peace Corps assigned me to a fish culture project in rural Zaire, Africa. About six weeks after graduation I left home for the first time from my family of twelve and flew to Auburn, Alabama for countless injections and an introduction to our project. After a couple of days, the group of us flew to New York and on to Africa for four months of fishery and language training as well as orientation to our new culture. Finally, we became Peace Corps Volunteers and began our job of teaching fish culture techniques to Zairian village farmers.

A little over one year into my three years of work, I wrote my mother and father and asked them to save my personal letters home, since I wasn't keeping a daily journal on the job. Unbeknownst to me, my mom had already started to do so, and kept the letters I wrote to some of my siblings as well. After I returned to the States, Mom never told me she had kept the letters, and I never asked. Then in September of 2001, one year after my mother's death as we were cleaning the home place for sale, my sister, Rose, made the discovery. In a tucked-away file were some 130 letters, perfectly arranged in chronological sequence.

As I reread these letters for the first time, I was reminded of the optimism, altruism, and compassion that a young person can have. These letters tell the story of a twenty-one to twenty-five-year-old man who wanted to help. Over the course of these years, the complex story of life in a developing country unfolds while a vigilant pen corresponds with, and keeps track of, the home front.

Today, it seems that one hears only a constantly overwhelming and mostly negative narrative from overseas. My prayer with this book is that, in spite of the fearful newscasts, the American people might understand that there are countless needy people in remote corners of the world who can still benefit from what one person can offer. The kindly villagers who so graciously accepted and appreciated our assistance two-and-a-half decades ago are still there, one generation later. May we Americans never be so preoccupied with ourselves that we fail to consider what we might do for our fellow men and women.

—John Jochum
Delmar, Maryland

Chapter One
Cameroon
1975

July 14, 1975

Dear Dad,

This money order is to cover my July premium. I wanted to send some more money to help cover film developing, but someone who lost his wallet asked to borrow some, so right now I am short.

We're all doing our last minute shopping and getting ready to leave Auburn. I bought some vegetable seeds and marigold seeds. I hope the constant tropical day-length doesn't hurt the flowering.

Have a good trip to Nebraska,
John

July 16, 1975

Dear Everybody,

I'm in Victoria, Cameroon now. This is where we stayed last night and will stay tonight. We'll leave tomorrow for Bamenda, Cameroon. This letter will probably arrive quickly because the airport is nearby. Mail delivery will be ten to fourteen days from Bamenda.

The flight went from Kennedy to Dakar to Monrovia to Abidjan to Cotonou and finally Douala. It was a nice flight along the coast. I had some short conversations in French with a few natives. I'll be glad when I can speak more.

The hotel here in Victoria is fantastic. It's built right next to the beach with very lush vegetation all around. It's the rainy season here, and it really rains. We had three to four inches from 10:00 last night to noon today. It's raining off and on

21

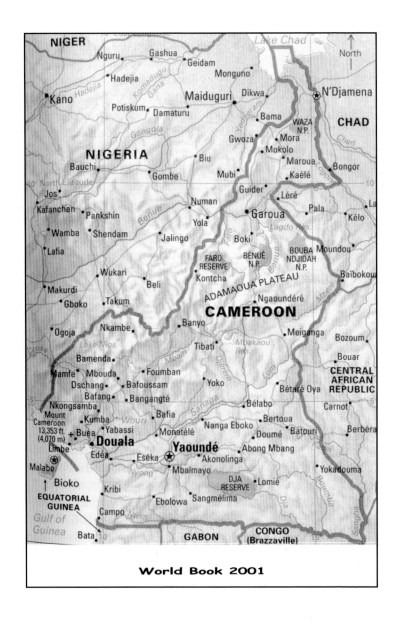

World Book 2001

now. I suppose it will be another downpour tonight with a lot of wind and noise. It's very relaxing.

The people here speak Pidgin English. It's mostly English, but word usage, syntax, and the accent are all a little different. Training will be in anglophone Cameroon also.

It's strange staying in motels all the time and eating at restaurants. I'm used to doing a lot of things for myself, but for the next two years many of my chores will be done for me, especially if I'm in an area of high unemployment.

We walked through town earlier today. The business district is similar to the Ocean City boardwalk in that there are many small shops one after the other. But these are all made of wood with tin roofs and usually wood floors—some were dirt. Shoes, cloth, cosmetics, food, and leather goods were common. I bought a pair of flip-flops for 250 francs, which is $1.25. I think I should have dickered some more and I may have got them for less. Two hundred Central African francs equals $1.00, so this letter costs $.40 for me to mail.

From the market I walked back along a road next to the black, rocky beach. A local who speaks English walked with me and pointed out some plants and places of interest.

Driving around here is fierce. There are no traffic signals, lane markers, or anything like that. You drive around potholes and try not to hit people, motorcycles, or trains that come down the center of the bridge with you alongside. Far more volunteers are injured by motorcycle accidents than all other causes of illness combined.

The dorm in Bamenda will be primitive compared to this hotel—no electricity or running water, and only outdoor latrines and showers. It should be an interesting change.

The return address may be better than the Yaoundé one. You could try it.

Hope all is well,
John

July 16, 1975

Dear Everybody,

This is the second time I've written to you today; however, I already mailed the first one home, and I just realized you won't be there, so I'm writing another one. I'm fine except for my right arm. I received a typhoid shot today, and it's sore now. It should go away in the next few days.

Garr Novick, the volunteer from Boonsboro, Maryland, whose father died last week, will rejoin us tomorrow or Friday. I'll send his address home when I get it. Maybe some of you could pay them a visit sometime.

(I'm in Victoria now—drove here from Douala yesterday.)

We leave at 8:00 AM tomorrow for Bafoussam where we'll spend tomorrow night and meet some volunteers. Then on Friday we'll go to Mbengwi (near Bamenda) for the fishery, and some French and cultural training. I'll be glad to settle into one place for a while instead of always unpacking and repacking all the time.

I hope you get this letter before you return from Nebraska, and I guess you'll have to wait for the other.

Enjoy your vacation,
John—En Afrique

P.S. The Bamenda address is better.

July 20, 1975

Dear Mom, Dad, et les enfants,

I'm finally settled into Mbengwi. I'll be glad to stay in one place for a while and get things organized. We start training in earnest tomorrow. Our daily schedule is: 6:45 breakfast; 7:30–12:30 fish culture; lunch; 3–5:00 French; 5–6:00 fish culture; dinner; 7:30–8:30 cross-cultural. We're off Saturday afternoons and Sundays.

Cameroon is an extremely beautiful country—far prettier than anything I imagined. There are many mountains, valleys, and rolling hills. The countryside seen from the fish station is very distracting. Mountains all around are covered with grass, rock outcroppings, and a few trees. The lowlands are forested and almost all the upland is under cultivation. The typical trees are banana, plantain, raffia palm, coconut palm, oil palm, eucalyptus, and many I don't know yet. The elephant grass is ten feet tall, so you always stick to the trails whenever you walk anywhere.

I would have had a roll of film to send home, but I threaded the film wrong so I have to start over again. Maybe by next Sunday I'll send a roll home.

I've been very lucky in that I haven't been sick yet. Many of the guys have had fevers, chills, shakes, thrown up, or had diarrhea. It takes a while to get used to different water, food, and airborne bacteria. But not even the five-hour time change has bothered me. I suppose my turn will come soon. However, many other PCVs told me they never were sick.

The house I'm living in is very typical for this area. It's a mud-block house with a painted plaster front. The inside wall of my bedroom is just mud block and mortar. My ceiling is the roof, which is metal and is supported by eucalyptus cross beams. The living room has a ceiling, which is a type of wallboard.

This is the second house the trainees are staying in. Seven of the fifteen are here. I have two roommates: Paul Olson from North Dakota and Jeff Towner from Ohio. We're just using the second floor in this house, so no one is downstairs. Up here we have a plank floor. Most houses are single-story with a dirt floor.

My bed is extremely comfortable. It's made of raffia and has a three-inch cushion. Raffia furniture is very inexpensive around here. A good bed is around $3.

We have no electricity or running water, but that doesn't pose any real problem. We collect rainwater off the roof in fifty-five-gallon barrels. It rains every afternoon so there's plenty of water. During the dry season we'll have to get water from streams and boil and filter it. There's a raffia shower stall behind the other house. We're having one built here. We fill a five-gallon shower bucket with water and hang it up on a rafter. It's no problem at all to take a shower, just pull the chain and water comes out, just like the pool back home. Cold showers aren't too bad really, but we could make a fire and heat some water if we wanted to.

We have two raffia and thatch-enclosed latrines at both houses (just like Boy Scouts, Jerry). They're no problem to use during the day, but it's a little tricky at night. For lights we have kerosene and propane lanterns. They're quite adequate; it's no problem to read or write. Light is from 6:00 AM to 7:00 PM, so we usually play cards after dark. The days remain fairly close to that schedule all year.

A few days ago Doug Tave (Chicago) and I were walking to the houses from the fish station when we met a local farmer. Like any farmer, he's very proud of his land and gave us a grand tour. (We're in anglophone Cameroon, so communication isn't too difficult.) Their system of agriculture is very interesting, and quite a bit different from ours. The land is piled up into one-foot furrows, about three feet apart. Unlike mechanized agriculture, everything is grown together. Corn (maize) has beans growing up it. Peanuts (ground nuts), cassava (manioc) yams, okra, tomatoes, and several others are all growing together on the mounds. The bottoms of the furrows are empty, both for passage and drainage. Because the soil is poor, each plot of land is abandoned every few years, and left wild. This allows some minerals and organic matter to accumulate. The farmer (Jacob) gave us two ears of corn each. People here are very friendly, outgoing, and generous. I'm looking forward to cultural and language training. Their traditions are interesting, and there's much I must know.

Still traveling back to the house, our next-door neighbor stopped us and invited us into his house. He had his wife fry up the corn for us. You just set the corn right on the coals, and as it burns (browns) you slowly turn it. To eat it you peel the kernels off the ends with your hand. They had a good laugh when we tried to eat it like corn on the cob.

Hope all are well there,
John

July 27, 1975

Dear tout le monde,

Our first week of training here is over; it has been quite a week. We have not been given any fish literature yet, and we have to figure out everything for ourselves. We were all given a pond filled with water, and we have to raise fish in it. The first thing we did was drain the ponds and harvest the "Tilapia" (type of fish we're working with) in it.

My pond was the first to be harvested, and we did it all backwards. We seined it twice, removed about 200 fish and were stuck in the mud. Now we seine five or six times before draining all the water out.

After draining the pond, I had to build the "monk" back up and refill the pond. A monk is a concrete structure used to regulate water depth. Boards are placed down the slots to whatever depth you want, and clay is packed in between. It's re-

ally efficient, but concrete is pretty expensive. A lot of ponds are drained by just digging a hole in the dam. Other people use bamboo pipe.

After filling the pond, I had to decide how many fish to stock. It was pretty tough not having any literature to base a figure on, but that's the way this program is set up. It doesn't require much thinking to read a book and follow directions. So, without any references, we are being trained to sit down and figure things out for ourselves. So we have fifteen different ponds and fifteen different management plans. It's quite an experiment, and the results will be interesting. Stocking rates vary from 120 to 10,000 fingerlings. I stocked 200 fish in a 250-square-meter pond. I was just talking with a fisheries volunteer who has been working for one year. He says he stocks one fish per square meter, so maybe my estimate wasn't too far off.

I just received your letter and the bank form yesterday. Yaoundé is quite a ways from here, and delivery is only when someone comes here from Yaoundé. Two weeks isn't bad, though. If you use the Bamenda address, it probably won't take long at all.

Steve Anderson, the fishery's director from Kikwit, is up here now, so I have my Zaire address. It's:

John Jochum, fisheries PCT
B.P. 199 Kikwit
Bandundu Province, Zaire

I believe this is both my training and job address. After I finish training in Kikwit, I'll become an official P.C. Volunteer, and the PCT will change to PCV. I'll be in Kikwit around the first of September.

I was glad to hear Jim and Tom both received scholarships. Maybe they won't have to work during the school year. That would make things a lot easier.

I hope your vacation was nice. It probably was pretty hot, though. It was 110 degrees once while I was in Nebraska in early July 1973. I'm sure Ann's thrilled staying out longer and flying home. I've had enough flying. You see more on the ground.

We had a couple of formal visits this week. Met what would be the County Director, the Delegate of Agriculture for Western Cameroon, and the Secretary General of Western Cameroon. Everybody was very cordial, and is behind us 100%. It makes you feel good to know someone in authority appreciates your efforts. I hope it is like this in Zaire.

This morning Garr Novick and I went for a walk. We followed a path from the fish station and thought we were heading for a monastery. We wound up at a public school, and the principal gave us a grand tour. They have English, French, history, geography, chemistry, biology, physics, math, social studies, and agriculture with fields for the students. It's completely run by the Cameroonians and it's rapidly expanding. It's good to see such a dynamic institution available for the local youths. Afterwards, Mr. Tata, the principal, drove us to a local bar for a couple beers (very traditional), and then gave us a ride back to the station. Everyone here is so open and friendly, it's really nice. The typical greeting is "You're welcome."

Hope all's well there. I haven't been sick yet.

John

August 3, 1975

Dear Everybody,

I received Mom's first letter from Uncle Ed's—only took nine days. It sounds like it was a good trip. I hope you had no problems coming home. I'll mail a roll of color prints home this week. I've had a little trouble with the camera. I hope they turn out.

We've been working on making and repairing nets, as well as surveying this week. Time is really starting to fly; only four more weeks here, yet we have miles to go. I'm glad I took French at Maryland—I'm quite a bit ahead on that. We have two hours a day the six weeks here, and on a scale from "zero" to "five" we're supposed to be at "one-plus" by the end of this six weeks. I'm already a "two" so I'm doing a lot of tutoring. I still have a long way to go, and am looking forward to speaking well. In Kikwit we'll have six hours per day in language class.

All this week a "Cry-Die" ceremony (funeral) has been going on. I went to it a couple of times, and it was very interesting. Many people were dancing, blowing whistles (flutes), pretend fighting with spears and guns, playing drums (hollowed logs, some with stretched leather covers), and firing blanks with their flintlock rifles. It's quite a celebration with drums pounding for a week after an elder dies. They really appreciated it when any trainees came. They gave us cola nuts, which is an African symbol of welcome; "mimbo," or palm wine; and/or a bottle of beer. You have to be discrete about taking pictures here. You can even have your camera confiscated in some areas. For this reason I didn't take any pictures of the celebration, but I found out later that I could have brought it.

By the way, in any letters or especially packages, never joke about spying or national policy. Any of my mail could be opened, and one volunteer was kicked out of Cameroon because of a facetious remark about spy equipment.

This morning a bunch of us went to a monastery with a local friend. A High Mass was offered and the music was very interesting with drums, guitars, castanets, and monks singing. The whole thing was rather formal and lasted around an hour and fifteen minutes. I think I'll tape some of next week's celebration.

After Mass, a couple friends and I toured the grounds. There were dairy and beef cattle, poultry, swine, and two horses. A complete metal shop, a cement-block manufacturing setup, and a photo-developing lab are all moneymakers. There was also a large vegetable garden. They're fairly self-sufficient, yet they provide a lot to the local people.

This afternoon a friend and I walked up a mountain and had quite a view of the area. It started to rain halfway up, so a local let us sit in his house for a while. Again we were offered cola nuts. They're bitter, but I pretty much like them. They're loaded with caffeine, though.

The weeks are very busy and I have few hours to myself. Whenever I'm not in class I'm reading or studying French. It's a good program and I'm learning a lot.

Happy belated birthday, Tom.

Hope all are well,
John

August 3, 1975

Dear Jerry,

Thanks for the letter. Your typing is pretty good. I received the letter August 1, so it took twelve days to get here, which isn't too bad.

I hope you passed junior lifesaving. You probably were one of the better students.

I bet you had a great trip to Nebraska, O'Fallon, Omaha, and wherever else you went. In 1964 we went to Nebraska when I was your age. I remember always having a lot of fun. At that time Hessie and Colleen still lived on the farm where Dad and his brothers grew up. There sure are a lot of friendly people there.

I'm learning quite a bit about fish: what to feed them, how to grow a lot of algae (phytoplankton) in a pond, water quality analysis, surveying, dam construction, predator control, and on and on. I have my own pond, which is twenty meters by twelve meters. There's a lot of phytoplankton and I put 200 fingerlings in the pond.

There's a lot of wildlife here: crows with white necks and chests, kingfishers, lizards, snakes, toads (big ones), insects, and a lot more. The big game (elephants, lions, etc.) is in the national parks. Maybe when I have a vacation I'll go there.

I guess by the time you get this, school will be almost ready to start. Try your best and blow that horn.

A bientôt, mon frère,
John

August 3, 1975

Dear Bob,

Happy Birthday—I hope this isn't too late. How has your summer been? Are you the champ at ping-pong?

Out here we do not have four seasons: winter, spring, summer, and fall. Instead, there are only two—the rainy season, and the dry season. Right now in Cameroon it's the rainy season and it rains every afternoon. The sun is usually shining until around 2:00 PM. We are at an elevation of around 4,000 feet, so it never gets hot. At night it gets real cold, around 60–65 degrees Fahrenheit. You can even see your breath.

The children around here make their own toys. I've seen stilts, pogo sticks (no spring), and hoops that you roll with a stick. The neatest thing I've seen is a stick-cart used to carry small things. It looks like this:

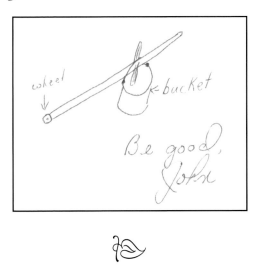

August 10, 1975

Dear Jochums,

Hello, hope everyone's fine. I'm still OK. We had a bunch of the flu virus going around. Four of the guys in this house had it pretty bad. One of my roommates fainted while we were doing some surveying. Everyone's OK now, though. I sure am lucking out—I've barely had even a sniffle.

This week we surveyed a water canal for a fair-sized pond complex. We had to go through elephant grass, forest, swamp, and general bush for five hundred meters. We had a local help us cut the bush with a machete. We called him the "country cat" (Caterpillar bulldozer).

Five of us built a monk for a local farmer this week. We'll take the forms off tomorrow; I hope it doesn't crack. After we finished pouring the concrete, the owner invited us into his house for some palm wine (mimbo). It tasted pretty bad when I first had it a few weeks ago, but I'm slowly acquiring a taste for it. It tastes like baking soda in carbonated water. They tap raffia palm or palm oil trees and let the juice flow into a calabash (a gourd). Inside the calabash, the juice will ferment with natural yeast. If the palm is tapped in the morning, the wine will reach full strength by the next day. I've never had day-old palm wine, so I don't know what it's like, yet.

We've finally been given the opportunity to use the references they have here, so I'm finding out all the things I'm doing wrong with my pond. We've all been assigned topics to give a seminar on. This Wednesday, Doug Tave and I will give our seminar on water quality. I've been doing quite a bit of work on it and am almost finished. We'll talk about oxygen, carbon dioxide, nitrogen and carbon cycles, pH, temperature, alkalinity, and buffering systems; not that I know much of anything about those.

This weekend the group of us went to a tourist hotel in Bali. It was mostly just for a break from Mbengwi. But it gave the cooks the weekend off, and us the chance for a hot shower. This morning I went swimming in a dammed-up creek they had there. I sure enjoyed that. I had to work on my seminar after that, though, which was too bad because I could have gone horseback riding.

My fishery training is now half over here at Ku-Bome Fish Station. I certainly don't have much confidence yet, but I suppose I've learned a lot.

My first roll of film was mailed Friday the 10th. I hope you get it all right. Mail sometimes doesn't make it through.

Sorry about this red pen, but all of my other pens either broke or were lost.

I suppose Ann will be home by the time you receive this. I'm sure she had a good time in Nebraska.

Love,
John

August 17, 1975

Dear Everybody,

It's too bad I gave you that Yaoundé address. We only get mail from there when someone comes up from Yaoundé, which is fairly far away, so no one has come for two weeks. Some people will be coming this week at least.

This week was really busy, and as we approach the finish

here, things get more and more busy. On Monday, we pulled the form boards off the monk mold. However, we didn't pour the concrete correctly, so we pushed it over and made a drain out of it. On Friday we poured another one. We'll find out tomorrow how good it is.

On Wednesday I gave a one-hour-and-forty-five-minute lecture on water quality. I discussed temperature, turbidity, oxygen, nitrogen, and phosphorous. My partner handled the carbon dioxide, pH, alkalinity, and hardness. It took a long time, but it went over well.

Yesterday we all went on a field trip to Ndop Fish Station to look it over. Afterwards we went up to the top of a mountain and visited a Fulani compound. I don't know much about the Fulani, except that they live up in the hills and raise cattle and horses. The view from up there was spectacular. I'm still amazed at the beauty of Cameroon. I went horseback riding, too, while I was there—bareback. I almost fell off once during a gallop. I had to grab hold of the neck real quick. I took a few pictures up there, so I'll finish that roll on the way to Zaire and mail it from there.

All my time is in fish culture and French language tonight, tomorrow, and until I leave. We were hoping to have a football game today, but everyone was busy—maybe next Sunday. I wish we had another two weeks here. We've learned quite a bit, but I feel we have a long way to go in a week and a half. I hope I'll learn enough to do a good job.

There are two two-year-old kids who live next door who are really cool. We've taught them to say "Ya-ba-da-ba-doo." Now they greet us with that as well as "Asha" (pidgin), "Ooh-ah" (African), and "Myaka" (local), which are all forms of greeting. They also give us five now. We're teaching another group of kids some nursery rhyme songs, like "This Old Man" and "Baa-Baa Black Sheep." They really pick them up quickly—quite attentive.

Hope all are well. I guess Jim and Tom have started school by now. Bonne chance mes frères.

Love,
John

August 24, 1975

Dear Jim,

Congratulations on your scholarship. I know that will make financing a lot easier. Good luck this year. Tell Mom I received her letter of the 17th of July this past Tuesday, one week after her letter dated July 23 arrived. Mail is weird. I hope Zaire isn't worse. On Thursday I received a letter from Leslie. As it happened, I wrote one to her and Mary the day after she wrote to me. Please thank her for me for it. Mom wrote saying you're thinking of going to Nebraska next year. I hope you'll find the time; it's a great experience (especially if you have a motorcycle), and a lot of fun.

If you've received my previous letters, you've read about the monk construction a group of us has been working on. Our first one wasn't any good, so we pushed it over. This week we finished our second and at least it's OK. This past Friday I harvested my pond. My fish (Tilapia nilotica) gained 1,900g during the four weeks, and I even made money, for my expenses were less than my harvest value. Four weeks is too short a time, though, to run much of a fishery experiment. I suppose when I finally get stationed I'll be able to run a few experiments. I did learn a lot of management practices on my pond, though, and along with seminars, lectures, and looking at ponds around here, I know a lot more than when I started.

Today we had a big football game. Basically, it was the guys going to Zaire vs. the guys staying in Cameroon and the staff. It was a lot of fun. I was really racked up once, though. I was trying to tag the runner when I was blocked from the blind side, flipped over, landed on my back and banged my head. I was OK. We won 2 touchdowns to 1 on a touchdown on the last play. After the game we had a roast pig on a spit for dinner. It was really good.

This Thursday we'll leave here for Douala, Cameroon, and leave there Friday for Kinshasa, and finally arrive in Kikwit on Monday. Time sure is flying fast now. It doesn't seem like I've been gone almost two months.

In general, the people in this part of Cameroon are pretty healthy. The diet is protein-deficient and many of the kids have the potbelly of kwashiorkor and internal parasites. But they grow out of it, and the younger adults are fairly well built. I don't know what the infant mortality rate is here, but I don't think it's very high. The diet is fairly well varied; peanuts are a common source of protein. Meat might be eaten once or twice a week. The diet in Zaire is far more restricted to cassava, which is almost all starch. I hope we'll accomplish something with fish culture.

Let me know how your summer finished. Good luck in school (if you need it).

John

August 27, 1975

Dear Mom,

Yesterday I received your letter #6. There was no problem with the Yaoundé address. I'm only missing the letter from around August 7. The mailing system here is not up to par with the U.S., and you must expect at least a month between the time you send a letter, until I receive it, and you receive one back. One of your letters took one month to get here, another only nine days. So, if you or I receive a letter at all we should be grateful, and if delivery takes less than two weeks, we're lucky.

I cannot mail APO from here, and I don't know if I mail it direct to Crailsheim, Germany, if it will get to Joe. I suppose it would.

I leave Mbengwi tomorrow from Bali airport. We'll fly in a twelve-seater to Douala, and on Friday we'll fly to Kinshasa. We'll spend the weekend there and fly to Kikwit on Monday.

We're all pretty excited about getting into Zaire. However, it won't be nearly as well developed as the N.W. Province here in Cameroon. I know that there will be quite a difference.

Now to answer your questions:

1) I'm plenty warm at night. I have a nice blanket.
2) The bananas here are the same as in the U.S.
3) We've had plantain quite often. It's sliced at an angle and fried in palm oil. They're quite good, similar to banana but not sweet. You'll find plantain from time to time in grocery stores back there.
4) We still eat American food for the most part, even a couple of birthday cakes. We have an *administratrice* (female administrator) and three cooks who handle the kitchen work. We've had foo-foo, which is similar to thick grits formed into a ball. You boil water and slowly add ground corn or cassava (tapioca is a byproduct of cassava) and some spices until it's nice and thick. You can eat it with a fork or your fingers. It's OK but most of the guys don't like it. It has very little nutritional value anyway, just starch. Another food that I like is jam-jam. It's a chopped up greens and meat dish with a bunch of other stuff. It looks awful but it tastes good.
5) There are reservoirs around; there's one being built near here for hydroelectric power for Mbengwi. Most of the streams and rivers don't dry up during the dry season, and houses are usually located near permanent sources of water.
6) The larger cities, such as Douala, Victoria, Yaoundé, and especially Kinshasa, are just as modern as any American city. It's usually not a good idea to drink the water, though. The smaller villages simply use latrines.

Sometimes there are spigots built on concrete bases where artesian well water comes out, quite forcefully, too.

7) No, I did not tape the monastery music, unfortunately. But I'll have more chances for that. The problem is I feel like a tourist whenever I take pictures or carry a tape recorder around. I've bought a shoulder bag (very common) that I can carry it in and conceal it a little.

When and why did Paul change from DeMatha to Carroll High School? I guess I'm glad he did because I enjoyed Carroll quite a bit. I'm still well. Hope all is fine at the home front.

Love,
John

Kinshasa, Zaire - 1978

Chapter Two

Kikwit, Zaire 1975

missions, are ask...
as I c... but I'll...
I havn't enough t...
minutes outside of...
I had used my...
stupidly I left my nylon jacket in Idiofa. So
stood under a tree getting soaked and freezing f...
was in the middle of nowhere - not... village,
top of the savanna... very
the rain come down and thinking how warm wa...
usually stay. I was s... though
less than a mile away, I knew I shouldn't
lone tree during a storm but... would
death if I sat under a...
         The rain slacked off a bit s...
2-3 kilometers and the downpour returned so I

September 7, 1975

Dear Everybody,

Hope everything's fine—couldn't be better here. Kikwit is a nice town. It's very spread out, too. It even has electricity and running water, both of which are true luxuries around here. Supplies come upriver by steamer fairly frequently from Kinshasa. I should not have too much difficulty finding things that I need.

Mom, as of now I have received letters 1–4, 6, and 9; #9 being the first to Kikwit, and it only took nine days. I've also received one letter each from Bob and Jerry. I've sent one letter home per week plus one roll of film (I'll send a second roll this week). I hope you're getting most of them, especially the film.

The trip down here was most interesting. We flew from Bali (near Bamenda) to Douala on a Twin Otter. That's a twenty-six-passenger, mountain and tree-buzzing turboprop. We spent one night in Douala, where I bought a shortwave radio for 9,200 francs ($46). It's a Sony, and pretty nice. I can get VOA, BBC, and a lot of French stuff.

From Douala we flew in a French DC-8. The airline was UTA, a very nice flight. We arrived in Kinshasa on Friday, and left Tuesday, Sept. 2. Kinshasa is an extremely large, busy, modern city. After six weeks in the quiet bush in Cameroon, I wasn't ready for the noise and hustle of a big city. There were some twenty-five to thirty-story buildings that were fantastic.

We flew from Kinshasa to Kikwit in an Air Zaire 737. We had a hot dog pilot, too. It's a visual landing at Kikwit, so he had to drop to two hundred feet to see the ground to find the runway, which we buzzed at three hundred mph. Then the pilot made a sharp U-turn with the wings almost vertical, and landed still at above two hundred mph. I must say, that's quite exciting even in a fair-sized jet.

45

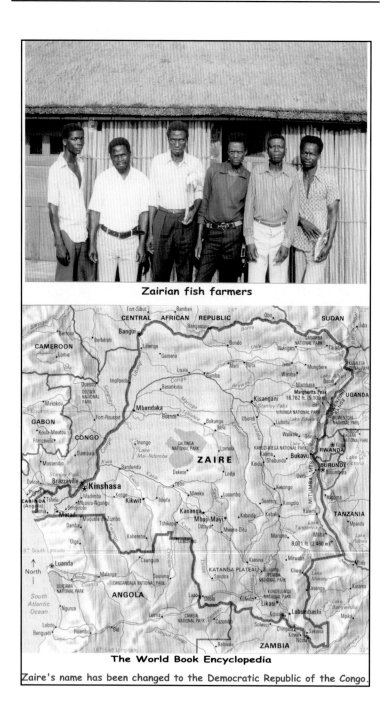

Zairian fish farmers

The World Book Encyclopedia

Zaire's name has been changed to the Democratic Republic of the Congo.

I'll send some film home this week with more on Kikwit.

Take care,
John

September 8, 1975

Dear Dad,

This is the second roll of film I've sent home. I hope you get it. As in the instructions in the first set of prints, please send copies to the McKinleys, to the Wrights and to Walt or someone else in Sutherland. Include with the prints the explanations that will follow.

I still haven't seen a single picture taken by this camera, so I don't know if it works well or not. They can develop black and white prints in Kikwit, so I've bought some black and white film. Now I'll find out if the exposure meter and everything else works.

Again, please keep a running account of what I owe you.

Thanks,
John

P.S. (September 10, 1975) Dear Mom, I received today your letter of the 3rd, only seven days—not bad. This was mailed the 11th.

Love,
John

September 14, 1975

Dear Mom,

I hope all is well—I'm still doing fine. As of now I'm only missing letters 5 and 7. I was really surprised when your letter of Sept. 3 arrived on Sept. 10. I mailed off a second roll of film this week.

We finally began our intensive language lessons this week (seven hours per day). It has been two weeks since our last French in Cameroon, so I'm glad to get started again. There are three guys in the advanced class, and we'll start the Kikongo tomorrow. I'm really glad I had French at MD. U. It's made this training a lot easier for me.

Yesterday we harvested the one operating pond at the fish station here in Kikwit. All the fish larger than four inches were sold to the people here. We kept about 500 small ones to restock, and the rest of the fingerlings were sold to local farmers for their ponds.

It was a riot during the harvest. People were there before we were, waiting to buy fish. They were probably waiting seven to eight hours before the fish were sold. They lined the banks as we slopped through the mud trying to net the fish. We harvested around seventy-five kilograms (175 pounds) of Tilapia, but that wasn't enough, and a lot of people went home without fish. They were sold for 80 makuta per kilo, or about $.80 per pound, which is a lot of money around here, where $2 per day is a good salary. The people really love fish. After we finished seining, about a dozen people went into the mud looking for stragglers.

It'll be great once we start working and teaching the farmers proper management procedures. You can grow more protein per unit area by raising fish than by raising cattle or most crops. It's a great way to improve the quality of the people's

48

diet, and because they enjoy eating fish so much there's a lot of enthusiasm in fish farming.

Wish my best to everyone. I hope everyone does well in school. In a way I'm still in school myself.

Love,
John

September 19, 1975

Dear Paul,

How's Carroll High School? I was surprised when Mom wrote saying you started there. She didn't explain why you decided to change from DeMatha, though. I don't know the situation now, but when I went to Carroll it had a lot more to offer the student than DeMatha. Needless to say Carroll has an excellent band, glee club, and "mask and buskin" departments. There are also a whole slew of other extra curricular activities. I'm sure you'll enjoy the glee club; be sure to try out for the plays. I think the most enjoyable times I had there were working with or being in the plays. High school doesn't seem that long ago to me. I hope your experience there will be a good one.

The schools around Kikwit are actually quite good. By 12th grade they're receiving advanced algebra and even some calculus. It will be interesting to see what happens when the well-educated take over the reins of Africa.

The Kwilu River is fascinating. Our program technical representative, Steve Anderson, owns a house with water frontage. About every other day we go into town so we can go swimming and wash in the river. The current is fairly strong so you can't swim against it, but you can keep up with it. So you can be swimming for five minutes but not go anywhere. Steve also has a small wooden boat in which we've ridden a couple of times. Pretty soon we're going to do some waterskiing.

Best luck in school,
John

September 21, 1975

Dear Mom,

I've received letter #10. It took nine days. All's fine here. In fact, I've been having a great time. Yesterday the new Peace Corps teachers arrived, and twenty-four of us had dinner at a hotel in Kikwit. Afterwards, about fifteen of us went to a bar, and we danced a little and drank a little.

There will be a lot of work during my stay here, but we sure have a good time whenever we get a chance. Steve Anderson has a tennis court in his backyard, and we've played a few times. I wish I brought my racquet. I've been doing a lot of swimming, too. I've swum across the Kwilu River (150–200 yards), and today I swam across another river, which was around one hundred yards wide.

We received some bad news yesterday, though. Pat Avery, one of the fishery guys who stayed in Cameroon, decided to quit the training stage and go home. Unfortunately, his father had died about two years ago, and his mother has been somewhat insecure ever since. He thought she'd be OK and his mother wanted him to take the opportunity to work overseas. But he decided, with difficulty, that he had better go home in case anything did happen. We're a close-knit bunch; everyone pulling for everyone, and it was very sad to hear about his predicament.

The other seven guys with me are Doug Medan, Bill Fiebig,  Mark Orlic, Dennis Murnyak, Art Locke, Kevin O'Sullivan, and Roger Palm. We all get along well and have had no personality conflicts whatsoever during the last almost three months.

Well, with birthdays and Christmas coming up, I thought I'd drop a few hints. Books have top priority, and I'd like a field guide on Western African wildlife, especially birds, insects, fish, trees, and flowers. I'd also like a map of the stars of the Southern Hemisphere. And, please send Grandpa's nameplate and those prints of those pictures I took at home just before I left.

I hope you had a nice visit with Mrs. Novick. I wonder how Garr's doing in Cameroon. Happy Birthday tomorrow, Ann.

Love,
John

September 26, 1975

Dear Dad,

I hope all is well with you and the rest of the family. I'm still doing fine.

Our language training is coming along quite well, possibly a little too fast, though, for the guys who never had French before. I sure was lucky to have studied French at Maryland U. I can pretty well explain fish culture in French. Unfortunately, though, few of the farmers speak French, which is why we're learning Kikongo.

I'm lucky Kikongo is a simple language structurally. The verbs aren't conjugated, and tenses are formed by simple prefixes or suffixes. It will take a while to learn the vocabulary, though.

This weekend we're going to Vanga, which is around 80–100 km north of here. Two of us will be stationed there. We're just going to look the place over, meet some of the local officials and farmers, and look at some of the ponds.

Next weekend we're going to Balungu to visit the last of the six sites. After that we'll decide among ourselves who'll go where. All of the sites are really nice. The people are friendly and enthusiastic, the countryside is quiet and beautiful, and there are more mal-constructed ponds to keep us busy than you can count.

At the Loa site and maybe a couple of others, someone will be in charge of constructing a full-scale fish station from the ground up. It looks like an extremely interesting job.

I consider myself very fortunate that I was given this assignment. The fifteen of us who were in Cameroon were chosen out of over one hundred applicants. There now is so much to learn between the fish culture, tropical agriculture, language, people, and on and on—it's an extremely rich experience.

Happy Anniversary, Dad and Mom. I'm sorry I'll miss the big one next year.

Hope your visit with Mrs. Novick was OK.

Love,
John

October 4, 1975

Dear Dad,

I received your letter of September 25 today, along with Mom's letters of the 19th and 25th. Mail service to and from Kikwit is pretty good. I'm going to be staying in Kikwit for the next two years, too. I'm glad to hear the pictures turned out OK. I've got 35mm slide film in the camera now. It'll take awhile to shoot up thirty-six exposures, though.

I received the bank deposit application while I was in Cameroon. I mailed it back, but I guess it was lost. That's just as well, though; you can keep the money in your account and use it to pay for developing costs. I never did receive the license renewal form. If you sent it to Cameroon, I might get it sooner or later.

Good luck with your new committee position with the town. I'm sure you'll enjoy it.

I guess I'll get back to Kikwit and explain my job. During the past several weekends we've traveled around looking at all the sites where we'll be stationed. As of last weekend we finished, and, during the week, we all got together and hashed out who'll go where. It turned out that I'm to be the manager

of the fish station here in Kikwit (Nzinda Fish Station). Only two of fourteen ponds are presently operable, so I have to direct the reconstruction of those other ponds, the water canal, etc. I have around twenty-five workers to supervise.

The Belgians built the station originally but went about it all wrong. All the dams have to be rebuilt, trees cut down, monks built, etc. As far as fish is concerned, right now I have to produce enough fingerlings to supply the other volunteers. After I get some more ponds into production, I can concern myself with food fish production for the local population.

Because I'm interested in fish culture as a career, this is probably the best site for me for the experience I'll gain.

Restez bien,
John

October 4, 1975

Dear Mom,

I'm up to date now with your letters except #5 and #7, which I don't suppose I'll ever see. I was sorry to hear you and Jim were having hay fever and bronchitis problems. I haven't had a bit of hay fever either here or in Cameroon.

Language is coming along quite well for me. The guys (five of them) who never had French before are having a harder time, though. I'm certainly not fluent in either language now, but I suppose after two years, I'll be pretty good at both.

It'll be interesting to read that tilapia article Jim found. There are several species of tilapia. We're working with T. nilotica. I just finished writing Dad a letter, and I was talking about what my job is here at Kikwit. But I didn't quite finish, so I'll do that now.

Last week a man from A.I.D. and a man from the U.S. Embassy were here to look at our project. They were the ones who provided the funds to buy our motorcycles (which we should receive next week). So, they wanted to see exactly what we were up to.

They were impressed with the work that has been done at Nzinda (the fish station) and see a great potential for both the station and the extension work we're going to do. In fact, they're going to provide enough funds and supplies (such as 1,000 bags of cement) to make Nzinda a full-scale station with storerooms, offices, classrooms, etc. I could very well be in charge of an extremely large construction project, and build something like the station where we stayed up in Cameroon.

I've just been invited to play a game of tennis, so I'm going to have to go.

Take care,
John

55

October 12, 1975

Dear Everybody,

I hope all is well and hay fever and bronchitis are going away. I'm still doing fine.

This stage is just about over, thank goodness. It really gets tiring to sit down and study all day, even if it is necessary. For the past two weeks, the three of us who had studied French before had four hours of Kikongo classes each morning and no more French. That gave us the afternoons to study vocabulary, which was helpful. I suppose in a couple months I'll speak fairly good Kikongo.

One of the local kids is hanging in the dormitory window watching me write this letter. He noticed I'm left-handed and thought it funny. I asked him what's wrong and he said, "Ce n'est pas bon, c'est mal." So I said "Pourquoi?" and he repeated the same thing in Kikongo ("Yo ikele mbi"). Their word for right arm is "diboka ya yacala" (arm of man) and left is "ya enkento" (of woman). It will be interesting to see how my workers take my left-handedness.

We saw Doug's and my house last week. It was night, so we didn't go in or walk around. But it's fair-sized with twenty-four-hour electricity and running water. It's right next to the edge of the plateau above the river valley. We'll move in this coming Thursday.

Friday evening was interesting. I was invited down to the little village that's in picture #20 of the second roll of film. This one guy there who has studied agriculture would like to work with me. We talked about it while drinking some palm wine and eating roasted peanuts. I don't do any hiring, so I don't think he'll work for me. Like everywhere else, kids like to show off, so the village children sang and danced for us. It was a lot of fun.

Take care,
John

October 19, 1975

Dear Mom,

I'm now, finally, an official Peace Corps Volunteer, no longer a *stagiaire*. We had our initiation last Wednesday night. Not too impressive really, a raise-your-right-hand-and-repeat-twenty-words-or-so-after-me sort of affair.

That evening we had a feast out at the Picnic Bar in Kipuka (nine km south of Kikwit). During the afternoons after class we'd go down there for a beer and to talk with the "patron" who wants to build some ponds. So we asked him to fix a dinner for us, and he came up with a good one. The entrée was goat. That was good—intestine, liver, kidney, the whole thing. We also had chicken cooked in palm oil, luku (boiled cassava manioc flour), fried manioc, saka-saka (boiled manioc leaves) "macaroni"—the young leaves of some plant still white and rolled up, similar to spaghetti, and several other things. All the volunteers in Kikwit (eight teachers and now the eight of us) were there as well as a bunch of other people. The acting U.S. ambassador was supposed to come, but he was busy. It was real nice.

Doug and I are the only two left in Kikwit. It was a little sad to see the eight of us split up after fourteen weeks. Everyone's glad to get out and start working, though.

We're living in Steve's house right now. Our house is in pretty bad shape. There's no electricity or water yet; all the wiring has to be redone; windows and screens need to be replaced; everything has to be painted; and the window frames, door jamb, and most of the doors are so torn up they should be replaced. The house has been abandoned for quite some time, so that's why it's so rough. Hopefully they'll get electricity and water next week so we'll be able to move in and start fixing things up.

I received letter #13, still fairly regular. If you haven't mailed the tennis racquet yet don't bother because I bought one from a volunteer who's almost finished. If you have, that's fine. I just hope it doesn't get stolen. Thanks either way.

Love,
John

October 20, 1975

Dear Dad,

Your letter with the renewal was finally forwarded here. I don't know if it'll be late or not. If you can't renew it, I suppose it doesn't really matter.

All is coming along OK here. Doug and I are buying supplies for our house. If they turn the water on, we could move in this week. We've hired a *domestique* (cook and house cleaner) and a *sentinel* who'll do all the lawn work. The sentinel (Tutu) worked for us out at Kipuka, so I know he's a good worker. He'll come around 4:00 in the afternoon and work until dark with the yard (about 5:45). He'll have a little spot on the porch where he'll sleep during the night.

It'll be strange having two workers since I'm used to doing things for myself. But it's good to give a couple of people jobs, and we'll have more time for fish work. They'll be paid around 18 zaires (about $36) each month. That sounds terrible by American standards, but it's quite good by Zairian. A farmer out in the country might see forty zaires a year.

John Kubarik has been the manager of the station for the past year. His term ends Nov. 10, so between now and then we'll be working together, exchanging ideas and so forth. I'll be working at the station only during the morning so my afternoons will be free. I hope to do some extension work ("vulgarization") with a few farmers. That's Doug's job mainly, but there's more work around Kikwit than both of us could handle full time.

My Kikongo's slowly coming along. It'll be nice to move into our own house and speak Kikongo with the domestique and sentinel. I suppose by the New Year both my French and Kikongo will be OK.

If you received my message not to bother opening a bank account for me, that's fine. If you never got that letter, just keep my money in your account.

Love,
John

October 26, 1975

Dear Everybody,

Hope school's coming along fine. I suppose everyone's doing fairly well. I'm still OK.

It's rather strange having to think about the fall back there and not being able to see it. The weather here is ideal. It might rain four times a week, usually in the afternoon or evening, and only for a couple of hours. If the sky remains overcast during the day, it stays cool to warm. When the sun's out, it's very intense. Standing in the sun is hot, though the shade is always cool. It has only been humid a couple of times. Most of the time it's fairly dry.

Doug and I are still living in Steve's house. Hopefully, we'll be able to move into our house later this week. The water was turned on yesterday, and hopefully the circuit box will be installed this week. Our domestique has been cleaning up the house and our sentinel has been working during the day fixing up the yard.

I've spent a couple of days at the station directing the workers. They all speak Kikongo—no French (malheursement). My Kikongo isn't too good yet, but I can pretty much tell them what work they have to do.

Along with the station I'm supplied with a Land Rover, which I have to maintain. It has around 80,000 kilometers on it, and is nearing death. We hope to get another one, somewhere,  somehow. We need it to haul feed and supplies, transport fish, etc. It's two-or four-wheel drive, and a lot of fun to drive.

Love,
John

November 2, 1975

Dear Dad,

All's still fine here, nice weather, too. I suppose nights are getting fairly cool back home.

We still haven't moved out of Steve's house and up the plateau into ours. They turned the water on, but we still need a fuse box, wiring, switches, etc. They are supposed to buy us furniture and paint, too, but I don't know when we'll see it. (The "they" is ultimately the Zaire government. We're working through a town official.) I feel fairly lucky, though; John Kubarik, the volunteer whom I'm replacing, never received a house of his own in his eighteen months here. He had to stay in other volunteers' houses. So even if it takes six months to get this house straight, I'll have at least eighteen months in it.

The station work is coming along very well. Even though John K. won't leave until Nov. 10, I've been going to work by myself, which gives me more Kikongo practice. (John K is working with the house trying to push the "kifumu" [chief] to get things done.) Two of the workers act as supervisors, so I take attendance and then tell Tayumbu and Mawango what I want done and they divide the work among the workers. Work is from 7:30–11:30 (usually 11:00) Monday through Saturday. If it doesn't stop raining by 6:30 in the morning there's no work that day. In fact, most of Zaire closes down when it rains. At any rate, my afternoons are always free so after I get settled in I'll do some extension work.

I hope the Loyola retreat was as nice this year as the few times I went there. I wish I could ride a bicycle here as I could there.

Love,
John

November 9, 1975

Dear Mom,

I received quite a few letters from home this week: Dad, Jerry, Paul, and the card—all on Tuesday, and your letter of the 23rd on Friday. I was sorry to hear all the sad news. Jim and I weren't close friends, but we saw each other quite often, especially at high school. It's strange when a person my own age dies. It certainly reinforces the fact that anyone can go at any time. I wrote to Kevin, and I hope they're getting along OK.

Question answering time:

No, I haven't gone to Gjuma (Jesuit mission) since that first time. It's over two hundred km north of Kikwit. Roger Palm is stationed there. There are two Catholic missions here in Kikwit; one across the Kwilu and one up on the plateau.

Whenever you send packages (generally the smaller the better) write "CADEAU" (gift) on the outside. I've been told they have a better chance of coming through then.

Dad, the Peace Corps should be taking out $14.71 from my readjustment allowance each month to pay for the policy. You might have to call them up and check on it. Also, I sent a $20 postal check home to cover one payment plus. I hope you received it. (Congratulations on your position with the life insurance company. Good luck.)

Local News:

Nothing more has been done on our house. I don't know when we'll move in. Soon I hope.

Station's fine, we're going to fill a second pond this week. I hope to have five ponds in production before long.

There are a lot of Americans in town. Thirteen Peace Corps people and a bunch of Inga-Shaba (hydroelectric dam) Power Line contractors. Their river port is next door to Steve's house. Last night we saw the movie *The French Connection*. Today, Doug, John K. and I were playing cards next door and were invited to a dinner of filet mignon, among other goodies. It's nice having a bunch of Americans around, but it makes it rather difficult to speak French, which I'd like to do more often. But I'm sure that will come.

Love,
John

November 16, 1975

Dear Everybody,

I suppose by the time you receive this letter, it will be around Thanksgiving. Hope you all have a nice one. We're not sure yet what we'll be doing; we hope to get a turkey off Inga-Shaba, but I rather doubt if that will happen.

We moved out of Steve's and up to our house this week. There's no electricity, so we use a kerosene lamp and charcoal stove. The house is in pretty rough shape, but it's livable. We'll get a garden going before long. We'll probably raise rabbits and maybe chickens.

Mom, I received your letters of the 31st and 2nd. I'm glad to see the pictures turned out OK. The tilapia article was interesting, but it didn't mention too much about Tilapia nilotica. Under good management we're looking for 2,500 kilograms of fish per year per hectare, which is around fifty pounds of fish from a ten-yard-square pond. That alone could double a rural farmer's income or be a substantial increase in the protein content of his diet. Fish ponds have a lot of potential.

A government agronome is supposed to come to the station, and I'm supposed to teach him how to manage it. I hope he gets here soon, for he will be able to handle the day-to-day things. I'll then have more time to work on larger construction projects at the station as well as some extension work. I'd like to get out of the city and into the sticks a little bit.

It's nice and cool here in the shade today, 70–75°. Hope it's not too cold back home.

Love,
John

November 21, 1975

Dear Sue,

How have you been? I am still OK. I hope you will be able to read most of this by yourself, but I suppose someone will have to help you a little bit.

Hopefully you will receive this letter before your birthday. Happy Birthday, six years old. How does it feel to be getting so old?

Do you like first grade? I bet you always have a lot of homework to do. Did you know that I, Joe, and all of us went to St. Ambrose? It has probably changed quite a bit, though, since I went there.

Today it is raining here, so I don't have any work. Nobody works outside when it rains. The rain is cold, and people would probably get sick if they got wet and cold. I think it will rain quite a bit from now until the end of December, so I don't think I will get much work done.

Once again, I wish you a Happy Birthday, and because Christmas is near, Merry Christmas.

Love,
John

P.S. Has there been any snow yet?

P.P.S. Dear Mom,

While I'm thinking about it, my completion of service date is October 15, 1977, so I don't know if I'll be home the 16th or not. At any rate, next year is your 25th anniversary, so I think it'd be best to celebrate it then. Hopefully I'll be there for the 26th, but I won't be sure for quite a while.

Love,
John

November 30, 1975

Dear Mom,

That was interesting calling home, pretty well broke my budget for December, though. We talked for thirteen minutes, which came out to twenty-seven zaires ($54). I think I can afford that maybe two times per year. We were quite lucky as it only took one hour to get through. Sometimes you have to wait over three days to make a connection.

As far as money goes, I'm earning 132 zaires per month. That's enough to eat well and even have an occasional treat. Have you heard that we are earning $125 per month back home? That'll add up to quite a bit in two years. Zaires cannot be changed back into dollars, and since I'm paid in zaires I can't really save money here. But, if I save 500 z, I can pay for my plane ticket in zaires, and the Peace Corps will give me that money in dollars. So, all in all, I can come home after two years with almost $4,000 in the bank. If I decide to work on a master's degree, that'll come in handy.

So far I've received all your letters sent to Kikwit except for Nov. 9. I've sent letters home every Sunday except last Sunday.

I sent Sue a letter on the 21st. I'd be interested in knowing what percentage of those letters made it through.

This week all eight fisheries volunteers are in town, the first time since we were initiated. It's really great to get together and see how everyone's doing. We had a meeting today discussing the project, what we've done and what we hope to work towards. Money and tools are a big problem. We hope to get funds from several organizations and get a supply of tools (especially shovels and wheelbarrows) that we can resell to farmers.

I've shot around one-half of a roll of color slides and I hope to finish the rest before long. I only have one more roll, so I'd appreciate it if you'd send me two rolls of ASA 80 to 160 35mm. Write "unexposed film" on the outside.

We're going to have a small harvest tomorrow in order to give some of the guys fingerlings. I'm a little worried; I just hope everything will go OK. It's my first harvest.

Love,
John

December 7, 1975

Dear Everybody,

Today was a big mail day for me: ten letters. Four were forwarded from Cameroon (Mom Aug. 20, Jim Aug. 24, Ann Aug. 25, and Bob Aug. 28). In the more recent bunch I received Mom's Nov. 6 and Nov. 24. As far as I can tell I'm only missing one letter from Mom from Cameroon. Earlier this week I received Dad's Nov. 19.

Thanks, Dad, for the info on U. of MD insurance. I'll check into it later. I haven't received any *National Wildlife*, yet, thanks for subscribing. I think that's the only magazine you need send, for between the other PCVs, Steve, and Inga-Shaba, I have quite a bit of reading material.

You asked me, Mom, what we ate for Thanksgiving. As I said on the phone, the day pretty much slipped by unnoticed. I think we ate pilchards and rice. We fired our first cook last Saturday because he was always late, and he took one whole day off because it rained. The next day we hired another guy, and he's fantastic. We've really been eating great. He's a superb cook, we even eat corn on the cob. Food is definitely no problem. The general menu is oatmeal and toast for breakfast; for lunch (dinner) we usually have meat (beef, pilchards, or corned beef), a vegetable (green beans or eggplant fresh or a canned vegetable), a starch (corn luku, mata-luku, or rice) and a salad (lettuce, cucumbers, radish, celery, onion). We usually have a fruit, too: pineapple, mango, papaya, or avocado. We usually don't have much for supper—warmed leftovers if anything.

Both lukus are usually made with manioc (cassava). Mata-luku is a sweet variety, you can fix it any way you fix potatoes and it's good, too. Luku is a general term for a flour mixed with boiling water until it makes a really thick glob. The Zairians love manioc luku and feel they can live on that alone, which is a big problem because there's no protein in it. We eat corn (maize) luku because it tastes a lot better and is far more nutritious.

The cook (Nquisi) also washes clothes by hand in a bucket and irons everything with a charcoal iron (a hollow, metal iron so you put coals on the inside). He's great, he gets here by 6:00 AM and we tell him he can go at 3:00 PM, but if he feels his work isn't done he'll stay until 4:30. I feel a little bad about paying him around 21 z per month, but that's around two and one-half times what the average Zairian earns.

The harvest last Monday was OK. We put around 300 fish in Steve's bathtub to hold them for two days to clean out their digestive system. But, the city has some kind of primary treatment, maybe chlorine, and we lost around 60% of the fish (which we ate, they were delicious).

I trust you did well on your exam, Dad. I suppose it's a little strange for you to be back in school, worrying about exams and all. I know I've had enough for a few years.

Take care, all.

Love,
John

December 11, 1975

Dear Tom,

How are things at the U. of MD.? How's bike riding? I hope you haven't fallen too many times yet. All in all, things are OK here. The house is still in bad shape. The Sous-Région hasn't done a thing for it yet. I suppose things will get organized sooner or later, though.

I have a slight leakage problem at the station. The former manager did not core the dams properly, so water isn't retained well at all. It will take a month to fix.

It's raining right now, there's no wind so I think it'll stay around for a while. People don't like to go out in the rain at all here. If it rains in the morning, businesses often stay closed all day.

Well, I hope you have a good vacation and Merry Christmas. Around fourteen PCVs of Kikwit are getting together for a Christmas party. It should be real nice.

Take care,
John

December 12, 1975

Dear Mom,

I don't remember how much I've told you about our dog (Boogie) and her seven pups, so I thought I'd give a progress report. Ten pups were born Nov. 6, but we killed three because we didn't think she could support all ten well enough. They're all big pups and have grown well. Two of them have had skin parasites, fly larvae that grow just under the skin. It leaves a hole as thick as a pencil and around an inch deep. They're healing up OK.

They're pretty frisky now, running all over the yard and crying all the time, too. We'll start getting rid of them next week. Three PCVs want pups, the rest we'll sell to Zairians for five to ten zaires. We might get a goat for one pup.

Big dogs are rare here. Boogie, at about fifty pounds, is the largest I've seen. We could probably get fifteen z per pup. Zairians in general don't take care of animals. Domestic animals have to scrounge around and fend for themselves (most are quite sickly). For that reason we're being careful about choosing which Zairians to whom we'll sell the dogs.

Love to all,
John

December 14, 1975

Dear Dad and Mom,

I hope you all had a nice Christmas. Mom, Happy Birthday. I'm not sure what will be happening here. In the evening (Christmas Day) all the PCVs in Kikwit are getting together for a dinner party. It sure doesn't seem like Christmas here, though. I don't think I'll be able to get much of a Christmas spirit, but maybe.

We're going to be working on a second fishery station. One of the Belgium doctors here is a friend of mine, and one day we were talking about providing the hospital with fish. From there we thought about the feasibility of building a series of ponds specifically for the hospital. As of now everything seems like it'll work, so we're now looking for a site. There's one valley two kilometers from the hospital that is a possibility.

The Land Rover I've been using has about had it. Both the clutch and brakes are worn out, the frame is cracked, and it has sundry other problems. Another L.R. is coming, but it won't be here for quite a while. In the meantime, I'm now using a 2-ton Ford pickup that came from the Inga-Shaba construction team. Zaire's pretty well broke, and so it can't pay for the Inga-Shaba power line. About 400 of 900 Americans have gone home, and a lot of equipment is idle. So, the fish station gets a big pick-up.

Good luck with the insurance business, Dad. I hope it suits you all right. I'm sure it's interesting work. Are you planning on working part-time until you retire from the Navy Dept.?

I've enclosed a few of my business cards. Some of the guys out in the bush say the farmers are really thrilled when they receive one. I've heard farmers have walked ten km just to get one of the guys' cards. *Pensez poisson* means "Think fish."

English words sound very funny to my workers. They all broke out laughing when I said their word *nedke* is pronounced *bird* in English. There are a lot of sounds in English that don't exist in Kikongo.

I wish everybody Christmas and New Year blessings. I only wish I could be there, too.

Love,
John

P.S. Thank you, Rosey, for your letter. It arrived today.

December 22, 1975

Dear Mom,

Thanks for sending those pictures I took. That guy at the camera shop gave me a bum deal when he said that first camera wasn't any good. So it cost me $75 to buy an identical camera just to fix the light meter. I'll probably send a third roll of film home shortly after Christmas. A week ago I mailed a package home to Sue. Let me know if it ever arrives.

The station has just received 300 zaires from A.I.D. I'll be using that to buy cement to build a water canal. This week I shot the canal and dam levels with a transit. We're building another sentinel's house because the old one caved in. As soon as they finish that, we'll probably get started on the construction of the canal.

Doug might be moving out of Kikwit. His extension work isn't progressing very quickly. I think Kikwit is too big and too full of white folk for rural people to find or even know about a fish culturist in town. So, he might move out into the sticks before long. There's a lot of work that needs doing, so it'll be good if he can go somewhere where he'll be slightly more busy. That might make living in Kikwit a little expensive for me, especially if I keep the domestique, the sentinel, and Boogie (the dog eats like a horse).

I'm going to make a couple loaves of bread for our Christmas dinner. I hope they turn out OK. It sounds like it'll be real nice. Everyone's making a little something. On Christmas Eve I'll go across the river and up to the Catholic mission's service along with a couple of the volunteers who live over there. I'll spend the night over at one couple's house. Supposedly, there is no Christmas in Zaire. (Mobutu has tried to get rid of Christianity trying to make Zaire *authenticated*. People are supposed to drop their Christian names for African names. At any rate, the people do celebrate Christmas but don't make too much noise about it. School continues until the 27th and I'm supposed to work, too. But several teachers and I aren't planning on going to work.

Merry Christmas, Happy Birthday,
and Happy New Year.
John

December 28, 1975

Dear Everybody,

Thanks for the care package. It arrived the 23rd, and I waited until the 25th to open it. It was great, even Jim's bubble bath. One thing, though, among other Western things, Mobutu has banned ties. So I doubt if I'll be wearing the one you gave.

Christmas Eve I went across the river and stayed at a volunteer's house. There's a clay court over there so I played a little tennis. We had dinner and afterwards went to the evening service at the mission. The mass was in French and the people sang in Kikongo. Needless to say I wasn't able to follow very much of it. I'll have to buy a French missal. After mass we visited a Belgian professor's house and had some beer and crêpes. They like to have a lot of candles burning for decoration. We talked for a while and then went home to bed.

Christmas Day I walked back across and up to the Boyd's house and made some bread (naturally) for the dinner. We had a bunch of stuff: curried beef, baked spinach and cheese, fruit salad, boiled cabbage, pineapple pie, and several other sweets. With all the volunteers from Kikwit there we had a great time. We hung around until 9:00, singing Christmas carols and talking, after which I went home to bed. It never really did seem like Christmas, but we had a good time anyway.

I might have found a site for the hospital's fish station. It's all overgrown with elephant grass, and I cut up my arms walking around the area yesterday. That tall grass is fairly sharp. We might get an agriculture PCV from Northern Zaire to work on the hospital's station. He has been there for two years and has recently signed up for a third year. During his vacation in the States, though, Zaire took his project away from him, so he might be free for a year to join us. I met him back when we were in Kinshasa. His name is Jim Jochum. He's from Iowa, so maybe he's a relative from way back when. If Doug does leave, and if Jim comes, he'll be living with me. That would be good, for I can barely afford to live by myself.

I guess there's not much other news. So, I hope everyone's well.

Bonne année (Happy New Year),
John

Chapter Three

Kikwit, Zaire 1976

January 5, 1976

Dear Mom and Dad,

I have received Dad's letter of Dec. 17 and Mom's letters of Dec. 16 and 23. I'm glad to hear Sue received her package so quickly.

Thanks for the journal, Dad. I'll let you know if it ever gets here. I should have all my tax payments refunded. I'm sure I'm below the limit.

Things have been fairly busy here lately. On New Year's Day (Bonne Année) around fourteen of us went out to the Picnic Bar (near the Kipuka stage site) for a Zairian dinner. With us was Gerald Ford's number two photographer (bumping elbows with some "biggies" over here). He's (Richard something) on vacation visiting his wife (Rosemary) who works in Kinshasa for U.S.I.A. (United States Information Agency). U.S.I.A. is going to do a videotape program on the fish project in March, so this was a dry run. (We're going to be famous!) It was interesting talking with Rich (who's around thirty) about the president and his day-to-day living. We also were brought up to date with Angola, the presidential candidate race, etc.

I guess being the only fishery program in all of Zaire makes us rather unique, for we were supposed to have some other celebrities come out yesterday to look at the station. A U.S. congressman and the American ambassador were going to come, but around Friday, the congressman decided to go to Angola instead (I suppose that's bigger news back home). (Pardon my mistakes. I waited too long during the day and now have to write by lantern.)

We have received some funds for the station: 300 z ($600) from A.I.D. for whatever I want (cement, right now). We hope to receive two hundred 50-kg bags of cement shortly from OxFam (700 z). I really need around five wheelbarrows and twenty shovels, but cheap wheelbarrows are 40 z apiece and

77

shovels are not to be found in Kikwit. If I can't find wheel-barrows I may buy plastic tubs. People always carry things on their heads and I think it would work quite well. They're "only" 4.50 z, so I might go ahead and do that.

Kikongo is no problem, all you have to do is get used to the sound and memorize around 1,000 words. My workers still tease me and say *Nge ke saba Kikongo ve!* (You know Kikongo not!) So I just tell them *Beno ke saba français ti anglais ve!* (You know French and English not!) I'm glad I know English already. It's complex compared to Kikongo. Whereas we have five pronouns to represent the first person singular (I, me, myself, my, mine), and the French have at least ten, Kikongo only has one, *mono*.

Thanks for Paul's picture. I will definitely mail the third roll of film home this week (five more shots to take).

Take care,
John

January 11, 1976

Dear Dad,

I've finally finished the third roll of film and will mail it along with this letter. If there are any outstanding shots, you could go ahead and send a few copies out to the relatives.

1, 2 Kipuka stage site.
   3 Our language professors.
   4 The eight fishery volunteers plus profs.

5 John Kubarik (whom I replaced—tall with beard), Steve Anderson (fishery program representative), Mr. Willit—in charge of training in Zaire.

6 Steve, Doug, Mark #'s 3-6 in Steve's backyard, October 15.

7 A couple of trees out by Kipuka, which impress me, their trunks are around five feet in diameter.

8, 9 Flies mating.

10 Palm trunk in my yard, there's a whole series of plants on the tree, lichens, moss, ferns, all the way to a small rubber tree.

11, 14 Village across the river from Kikwit.

12 Ville Basse Kikwit, downtown port.

13, 15 Chinese agriculture project, there are six Chinese here. They have around a hectare of vegetable gardens, which is great, for if they weren't there, vegetables would be hard to come by. Needless to say the bulk of their work is rice, hectares of it. They're really good farmers. We use their rice bran to feed our fish.

16 My backyard: papaya tree with fruit, a small oil palm, the partially built fence. Now there are palm fronds stuffed in vertically. The house in the background is a typical Belgian house; they like to mix all sorts of colors together. Rooms can sometimes have four walls, each with a different color.

17 Front of my house—sad-looking, isn't it? I think I'll be waiting two years before the Sous-Région will fix anything.

18 Crown of palm oil tree in front yard.

19 Pups. Boogie had ten pups, three of which we killed because we didn't think she could raise ten healthy pups. The remaining seven drained her. When we gave the last of them away she was nothing but skin and bones. She has put some weight back on now. She's a

stupid dog; I hope I can get her to come when I call
her by the end of two years.

20 One of the station's ponds. Notice the compost *lupangu* (enclosure); we put grass clippings in them.
It takes about a month to use up a full lupangu. The
water is nice and brown, which means there is a thick
zooplankton bloom. The water changes colors from
brown to green to brown depending on whether zoo
or phytoplankton dominates.

21 A pierced dam. Boards are placed in the middle slots
and clay packed in between. Unfortunately, John K.
didn't know how to build a monk form, which would
have been a lot better. A monk uses one bag of cement
to the pierced dam's five.

22 Water canal, ponds in construction, and bird's nest.
Hopefully by the end of this month we'll start pouring
concrete in the canal. The soil is too sandy to just dig
a ditch and run water down it, so we need around 400
bags of cement to construct one of cement (OxFam
and A.I.D. money).

23 Pierced dam again with H_2O in pond.

24 Hole in hillside—this is where we get the clay for dam
construction. Keep in mind all work is done by hand
(slow process).

25 Above the hole I noticed this palm tree. Below the
crown you'll find two calabashes. Someone is tapping
palm wine.

26 This is the stream (Nzinda Stream) where we empty
the ponds; at the head of the station it provides our
water source.

27 A bird that eats our fish. There are two of these birds
as well as some kingfishers that frequent the ponds.
As long as the ponds have a thick algal bloom, though,

the birds (as well as frogs and predacious insects) can't see the fish, so they don't eat too many.

28 The station as it was, and what I'll have to fix.

29 What has been worked on so far.

30 A patch job on a dam. The dams weren't strong enough and there are a lot of leaks. This job took two days for five workers.

31 The ol' Land Rover. It's about had it, there are no brakes, the frame is cracked, and on and on. OxFam is providing us with a slightly less-used vehicle. When, I don't know.

32–34 Harvesting (traditionally) and cleaning up the #1 pond (reservoir right now). No work has been done on this pond yet. I won't repair the dams until after the cement canal has been built. We only harvested one bucket of fish out of this pond, which isn't surprising since we didn't feed it (the pond).

35 Three types of fish. Tilapia nilotica on top, a predacious native fish, and another species of Tilapia (two of them). If well fed for two years, the nilotica will weigh over two kilograms. This one is around 150 grams.

36 The future site of the hospital fish station. The typical pond that you see is around six inches deep and the dams are filled with bamboo, leaves, and assorted other junk. Needless to say they can't produce fish. In the middle of the picture is a lady deepening a pond where she soaks manioc to get rid of an acid in the root.

I hope these photos all turned out OK. I think some might be unexposed again. I'll send some more home in a couple of months.

The Dixons sent me a Christmas present that I'm sending back to you. Because I lost my sunglasses and would appreciate it if you used this money plus some of mine to send me a pair of polarized sunglasses.

Last month I wrote this enclosed letter to the boss of the fish station. This is a Belgian-style business letter which I can't stand for it's twice as long as it needs to be. The French typewriter is pretty much the same as ours. The Q and A are reversed, the M is at the ";" and W, X, and Z are all mixed up. Other than that the letters are the same, plus there's é, è, ê, etc.

Doug moved south eight kilometers into a little village. No one knew why he was here before, so he moved to where he's the only *mondele* (white man) around. His work has already picked up. So I'm in the house by myself now, along with Boogie. It's nice and peaceful, and I'm able to settle down after the daily frustrations of trying to get a decent four hours' worth of work out of my workers.

I'm starting to do extension work, looking at my workers' ponds. I've seen three so far—two are worth working on. However, the owner of one of the ponds said he didn't want to feed the fish for if he did someone would steal them. I must admit that that does make fish production rather difficult.

I'm slowly getting used to always being stared at wherever I go. It's weird always being reminded you're white and different. At least I don't mind going to church anymore. It was rather difficult at first. I felt as if I was a sideshow at the circus. I'm getting to know some of the Belgian missionaries too, which makes things easier.

Wish Joe a *Bonne arrivée* for me. I hope he gets back into everyday life OK. [Joe, the oldest brother, had just completed four years in the Army.]

Love,
John

January 19, 1976

Dear Everybody,

Last week was a fairly exciting week for me. A lot of things happened.

My January, February, and March money hasn't come in, so I lied last week when I said I would be mailing film #3. However, I have had to borrow some money, so I'll mail the film this afternoon now that I can buy the stamps.

I changed my job description last week and I should have done it earlier. I really used to get frustrated by how slow the workers worked at the station, and felt it was up to me to put some enthusiasm into them. However, it's not my fish station, it's Zaire's. There's an agronome here who was supposed to have been doing what I've been doing for the past two months—that is, to see to it that the work gets done.

He never came out to the station for two months because he didn't have a jeep of his own. However, he could have taken a taxi. It wasn't until last Saturday that he wrote a letter to Kinshasa asking for a jeep.

So I got fed up doing his job, worrying about the station and him never coming. Last Thursday I gave him the attendance list, all the money left from previous harvests, and all the receipts of things I had bought. I told him my job was to give him the technical advice on how to repair the station and everything else was his problem, and unless he came to the station I wouldn't come and no work would get done.

So he finally started working and wrote the *état de besoin* (state of need) letter and is now coming to the station. I feel as if a burden has been taken off my shoulders not having to worry about the speed of the development of that fish station (Zaire's problem). Also, I now have time to work more on the hospital's fish station or even to go out *en brousse* and see what the other guys are up to.

What finally got me to tell the agronome off was a thief (one of the workers) who stole the two wheelbarrows and tried to drain one pond. It felt good to tell him to solve that problem.

Change subject.

Boogie's coming along OK. She has put on some weight since the pups all left. Her ribs only stick out a little now (versus skin and bone). She's still a little mixed-up for she has changed hands and homes many times during the last two years (almost). She's getting used to me (sole master now that Doug has moved south ten km) and the house. I hope before long I can train her to stay in the yard and not run off. I have a fence, but she gets through that easily. She likes to chase sticks. Since she's a big dog (around sixty pounds) I found a big stick for her (three feet long and five inches thick). I figure if I get her good and tired chasing that branch she won't want to go walking off somewhere.

Yesterday was a fantastic day. Three fish guys (Bill, Art, and Doug), three PCV teachers from Kikwit, two Inga-Shaba guys, and I went floating down the Kwilu River for four hours. An Inga-Shaba truck drove us upriver around fifteen miles where we unloaded ten truck inner tubes, a case of beer in an ice chest full of ice, and some munchies. We all climbed inside our own tube, hung on to one another's tubes, stuck the ice chest into the tenth tube and headed on out (9:30–1:30).

There wasn't a cloud in the sky. It was great. There isn't any big game around here, for the people have killed it all off (except for a few hippos, but we didn't see any). There are a lot of birds, though, and we saw ducks, cranes, swallows, kites, hawks, and some I don't know.

The current (around four to five mph average) swept us into two fallen trees, but we just bounced off and kept going. There was an ample supply of sunscreen; I'm just barely burnt today. I'm used to the sun for I'm in it every day. I haven't seen any of the teachers today, but they didn't look so good yesterday. I swam about as much as I floated, and between the sun and the exercise, my shoulders hurt so bad I couldn't sleep until I took two aspirin last night. There wasn't a bit of pain this morning, though.

From the time we entered the water until just above Kikwit it was nothing but dense, green jungle, vines and everything. We were probably the first whites ever to float down the river, and every now and then we'd hear a few hoots from the jungle. Whenever we saw someone, we'd ask them how far was it to Kinshasa. They'd just say, "yo ke entama!" (It's far away.) Once in a while someone would question, "Sambu na inki?" (Why?) It was great. We hope to make it a Sunday afternoon affair every week.

Love,
John

January 26, 1976

Dear Mom and Dad,

Sundays seem to get busier and busier so I have to write on Monday again this week. Mom, I've received your letters of the first and fourth of January. Dad, both packages arrived.

The star chart is great—thanks for finding and mailing it, Dad. A couple of nights ago a bunch of us were lying on Steve's tennis court looking at the stars. We found Orion, Canis Major, Canis Minor, Hydra, and Gemini.

ASA sixty-four film should be quite good for color. I don't take too many low-lighting shots anyway.

Yesterday, the U.S. ambassador, Mr. Cutler, and his wife and two children (two boys, fourteen and twelve), the P.C. Director for Zaire, and the pilot and engineer dropped by for a five-hour visit right here in Kikwit. They arrived at 10:30; directly after that we went to the Nzinda station to look at the "#1 P.C. project in Zaire." After looking at the station we went to Steve's house where we had lunch with the ambassador's group and all the PCVs of Kikwit.

It was an enjoyable afternoon. We all just sat around and chatted until 2:30. Mrs. Cutler brought some chocolate chip cookies that were quite good. Around 3:00 Steve and I drove them back to the airport.

Last week Steve was in Kinshasa for a budget meeting, and during that time they (the administration) voted that the Bulungu Zone Fishery Program is the best P.C. program in Zaire. Of around eleven programs, ours shows the most organization and potential. I hope we'll meet these expectations.

There's no news on my house. The Sous-Région has yet to do anything for it. I still don't have electricity, much furniture, paint, etc. I'm beginning to wonder if they'll ever do anything to help me fix the house. I've planted sunflowers, marigolds, and pineapple, and I'm now starting a garden.

I hope all are well and no one has fallen too many times ice-skating.

Love,
John

P.S. I just received Sue's letter of Jan 1 (mailed the 12th). Thanks for helping Sue, Jerry. I hope you've received the letter saying I received the package on Dec. 23rd.

February 1, 1976

Dear Everybody,

We've had a rainy week here this week. It has rained all morning long three of the past four days. A couple of times it has really stormed, with the palm trees leaning over to the wind and rain coming down in sheets.

I've got a thermometer now. It has only ranged from 70° to 80° with all this cloud cover. I think during a bright, cloudless day the temperature may reach 100°, maybe.

Because Steve Anderson has been on a couple of trips this week I've been doing a little of the regional representative's job. We have twice-daily radio contact with the P.C. office in Kinshasa, so I worked the shortwave. I also had to do some running around in various Land Rovers. I picked up the Ox-Fam rep for Zaire at the airport. He's looking at various health and ag. programs where he can (might) approve OxFam support. Our fish station is one possible area for funds. We hope to receive two hundred 50 kg bags of cement.

Work at the station is really progressing. The agronome is on the ball and has the workers jumping. They've finished one pond and will complete two more shortly. That will put six ponds (a little less than one acre of surface area) into production by the end of February.

I only have to go to the station for perhaps an hour each morning. It's nice just telling the agronome what needs to be done and how to do it. It's his worry now to see to it that the work gets done, and at last it is.

We'll harvest a pond completely tomorrow. Most of the fish will be restocked in other ponds. Any fish more than what I need for the station and what Mark and Doug want for their ponds will be sold. I haven't any idea how many fish are in the pond. I hope to sell thirty kgs of fish as food.

I'm invited to dinner tonight at the OxFam nurse's house along with Steve, Siri (his girlfriend visiting from Minnesota), and the OxFam director. (It was nice. I just came back.)

In my toe I have a mite that develops a pea-sized egg sack (which it has already done). So, I have to cut this small sac out of my toe. That's no fun, for it really hurts. It shouldn't be any problem, though, if it doesn't get infected.

Love,
John

February 8, 1976

Dear Mom,

I've received your letters of the 12th and 22nd of January. You asked a lot of questions, so I'll go through them first.

All of my cuts have healed up fine, including that mite in my toe. I have this white fungus growing on my shoulders and neck. Separate colonies are little white dots: when they become thick it looks like peeled, sunburnt skin with light and dark patches. It can't hurt you, but I'm treating it anyway.

The site for the hospital's station is still up in the air. The Sous-Région disapproved the first site. So we have to look for a second site now.

No magazines have arrived yet. I'll let you know when they do.

Boogie is coming along well. I've gotten rid of her fleas, and her coat looks healthy now. She has put on a lot of weight. She's becoming better trained as she gets used to me. I've taken her for a few walks without the chain and she stays by me. I took her across the river in a dugout canoe and she was real good. I had to pick her up to get her into the canoe, though.

I can make ends meet in my budget, but it's close. I can only go out to dinner maybe once a week. Maybe in two or three months I'll be able to make another phone call. I'm going

to build a chicken coop soon, though, and I'll enjoy raising chickens. I've heard rumors that Zaire is going to devalue its currency to one zaire = one dollar (nearer to the world market). That would more or less double my salary. However, inflation is extremely high here so even with devaluation, things might not change much.

Those curtains would be nice. Nothing has yet been done with the house. I'll see (maybe) the commissioner of the Sous-Région tomorrow and see where things stand.

Thanks for sending the stuff I asked you for. Don't worry about the stain, for I think I can use shoe polish. I hope things come soon.

I had a nice day today, played softball with four PCVs and three Inga-Shaba men and a few Zairians. That's a difficult game to explain in French or Kikongo. After that we had a steak BBQ. We might go tubing again next Sunday. They went last Sunday, but I unfortunately had work to do.

Love,
John

P.S. I'll have to buy a new pen—this one smears too easily.

February 15, 1976

Dear Mom and Dad,

This was a good mail week; received letters from Dec. 29 and Jan 15. I also received Jim's letter of Jan. 27 and the package with the parts and sunglasses.

Thanks a lot for the glasses. They make being outside a lot easier on the eyes. They look real nice, too. I'm afraid to say, though, that only the plugs fit the bike. It seems the U.S. does not import the Yamaha YB 100 and whoever sold Jim the points and condensers made an expensive mistake. So, we now must rely on finding parts in Kinshasa, which may mean we'll soon be walking.

I'm sorry to hear Mrs. Bowden's not doing too well. How is she now? I hope everyone else is OK.

Bobby, thanks for your letter, you write a good letter. You're right in that scales weigh fish, but fish have scales of their own, and what are these scales?

Yesterday and today we had our bimonthly fish culture team meeting. This time we had it up in Bulungu, a city 140 km north where Art is stationed. It was a good meeting. We got a lot of business done and exchanged a lot of ideas.

When I arrived Saturday and saw some of the guys whom I haven't seen since November, I was moved almost to tears. This was the first time since October that I got out of Kikwit. And by being here working for the government and continually fighting government hassles, I had forgotten why I came over here in the first place. Seeing the guys and hearing what they're doing, I remembered that I, too, had come hoping to help these people in a way all the other guys are doing. I've almost arrived at the point where I don't like the Zairian people because of all the frustrations I run into with the town administration. Therefore, I'll never let a month go by without visiting a couple of the guys "out there" and reaffirm the commitment I have to the Zairians. Hopefully, working with the government at the fish station will indirectly help the people in the future months. But I'm saddened that I'm missing the person-to-person contact with Zairian farmers. Hopefully this will ameliorate shortly.

Other than that, things are OK. I'm eating well and am still healthy. I'm the only volunteer I know who has not yet been laid up sick in bed. I certainly thank the Lord for that.

Love,
John

February 23, 1976

Dear Mom,

Your letter of the 22nd arrived along with Joe's and the tax form. I don't think I've ever been in a wind chill of -35°. That must be some winter you're having. My marigolds are flowering; beans, okra, and some other flowers are open; basil (green) is on the way; and I've got six more pineapple cuttings to plant. (Eat your heart out.) Just today a PCV gave me some zinnia (seeds) which I'll plant tomorrow. It's amazing how things grow here (including fungus on people).

I had another great weekend the past two days. I went to Loa (fifty kms – 90 minutes) to visit Mark (PCV fisheries) and told him I've completed the monk form (remember the monk). I was planning on returning directly home, but he told me to stay at least until Sunday, so I did.

I visited one of the farmers he's working with and took some pictures of his pond. He really has a nice setup and is producing good-looking fish. It was great tromping around *en brousse* again.

That evening we went down to Lussanga (fifteen kms but only fifteen to twenty minutes) and visited the Polish doctor and his Belgian wife along with two other

Belgians there (good practice speaking French). They were really hospitable.

We started out playing tennis (with four Zairian *boys* running around as ball boys—typically colonialistic). They're the best two (the Doc and Bert, an engineer) tennis players I've seen around here.

Right after that, we went swimming in the pool that was twenty-two-yards long with a diving board. I didn't think I'd ever see a swimming pool in Zaire, and it was great.

Then we sat around and chatted. At around 7:30 we started dinner: crêpes, soup, meat, and red cabbage and potatoes, and a dessert. We drank three different types of wine, one each for the appetizer, the soup, and the meat. They served all in style, one course at a time. I was terribly grubby, though, for I hadn't realized I was going to be there. I wore dirty jeans and a sweat-soiled T-shirt, and I hadn't shaved in four to five days. They didn't seem to mind, though. I think we reminded them of their kids in Belgium.

Directly afterwards, we started playing bridge (yes, I play bridge now, even in French), which we did until 3:00 AM. I only played two hands the whole night at a one and two bid. I averaged having three and four points in my hands—even saw a couple ten-point high hands. I had a good time anyway.

We slept until 9:00, had breakfast of bread, cheese, and coffee (typically Belge—light breakfast and lunch and a late, full dinner), swam some more, had a nice lunch, and at 2:00 we took off. I went with Mark back to Loa, and then back to Kikwit. It was a great time, and I know I'll be back before long.

Hope all are well,
John

March 8, 1976

Dear Mom and Dad,

I received your letters of Feb. 9, 17, and 25. The mail seems fairly regular. I've also received one copy of *National Wildlife* and one of *International Wildlife*. Those sure are nice magazines—everyone's reading them.

I finally received a letter from Joe dated October 8. (I hope your boils are better by now, Joe.) It came by boat from New York. (It takes more than a 10-cent stamp, Joe.)

You were talking about my house not looking so bad. Well, it could be fixed up all right. But I don't have the money to do it myself ($2 paint brushes cost 4.50 z or $9) and my sponsor (the Zaire government, unfortunately) doesn't have the money to fix my house either (so they tell me).

I suppose I'll be living in this rundown house for two years. I don't mind living like this at all. I was ready for less-fancy living conditions. What bothers me is the lack of government cooperation. After all, I'm here to help them, and I think the least they could do for me is give me a couple chairs and a table.

I don't think there will be another fishery PCV here after I leave in 1977. If I decide to extend and work an extra year or two it won't be in Kikwit.

I have no more fungus growing anywhere anymore. Due to constant high humidity, that'll always be a problem, though. I don't think swimming in the Kwilu has anything to do with it.

I have plenty of shirts, thanks anyway, Mom. I rather doubt if I'll even wear the clothes I brought over.

We received some good news concerning my job today. The agronome who has been more or less working at the station has been transferred. A former Zairian agronome has taken his place (thanks to Steve Anderson). Ngam (the new manager) has worked for the past year for Peace Corps here in Kikwit. Last month P.C. fired all Zairian assistants, even though Ngam was (and still is) highly needed. (However, Washington has spoken and budgets have been cut.)

So, Ngam is a personal friend of mine, and it will be a pleasure working with him. Plus, he is extremely efficient and conscientious so I know work will progress rapidly. This is really great for now. I'll be able to enjoy working at the station. Ngam may have the chance to go to the U.S. to study fish culture during the summer of 1977. I'll probably help him learn English and what little I know of fish culture at the same time.

Dad, I hope all your exams turned out OK. Best of luck with your plans.

Love,
John

March 16, 1976

Dear Mom,

All's well here. I've received Bob's and Sue's and your letter of early March.

My yard is coming along OK. The beans are growing well, and I have a bunch of other seeds to plant. Marigolds are blooming and zinnias are up. By the time you receive this letter there should be chickens in my chicken coop.

Last Wednesday, Steve, Ngam, and I met with the minister of agriculture for Zaire (#1 ag. man). We had an interesting discussion and are looking for more collaboration between the Zaire government and development organizations. He also hoped that our fish programs could expand to other areas. It all sounded well and nice, but I'll have to wait and see if he actually does anything.

We're still waiting for the formal letter stating that Ngam is assigned to the project and that the former agronome, Galason, is transferred. Things are moving so slowly right now at the station that I'm fairly well frustrated trying to work for the Zaire government.

Two PCVs from Kikwit and I took a truck to Lusanga Saturday. Had a nice dinner with Janis and Barbara (Polish doctor couple) and afterwards we played bridge until 4:00 A.M. Before we started, Janis said "au travail" (to work), which an eight-hour marathon of bridge almost is.

Take care,
John

March 16, 1976

Dear Bob,

Thank you for your letter. I hope you are feeling fine now. I have never been sick yet over here, not even the flu.

You are right; fish scales cover their body and protect them against cuts and disease organisms. The name of the fish I'm working with is Tilapia nilotica, and it eats phytoplankton and zooplankton. Do you know what phyto and zooplankton are?

What are you learning in school, Bob? I bet you're real smart and get 100s on all your tests. Do you ever walk to school? Here, almost everybody walks wherever they want to go because cars are very expensive and only the very rich people can afford to buy them.

Love,
John

March 22, 1976

Dear Mom,

Not too much news at this end of the road. Received your March 9 letter. I'm doing OK, healthwise. Hope everyone back there has gotten over all the flu, colds, sore throats, etc.

Work is almost at a standstill at the station. The government agronome never shows up, so there's no discipline left among the workers. I'm seeing more and more examples of where Zaire involvement in a government-sponsored development project means that the project is doomed to failure. If Ngam is not allowed to work with us, I think I'll try to transfer to another fishery site. Fortunately, the other seven fish guys are all coming along OK.

I hope to work with a Mennonite (American) mission here in Kikwit. They have a fair-sized agriculture extension project, and are doing quite well. They hope to build some fish ponds and have me teach some of their extension workers a little about fish culture. The American whom I hope to work with is out of town now. I will see him in a week or so and hope to get started.

Played bridge again yesterday up in Lusanga. Had a nice dinner, too. The Doc and his wife (a doctor, too) are most generous and friendly. The best dish was a Polish soup of cut-up cow stomach—delicious.

Love,
John

April 8, 1976

Dear Mom,

I'm sorry to hear you have had some more difficulties. I wish I could have been around to help you if I could. If you ever feel like writing some of your thoughts down, maybe it would make things easier to discuss them. I know it's not good to keep anxieties pent-up until they all at once explode. [My parents raised eight teenagers during the 1970s, so one can understand why there were a few trials in my parents' lives.]

I just heard from Dad that Jerry broke his arm. He's a year older than when I broke mine, isn't he? Wish him good luck and sign his cast for me.

At the house here things are coming along. My ten chicks are eating well. Maybe in three to four weeks I'll be able to tell how many hens and roosters I have. Being only five weeks old, they're too young to distinguish now.

Boogie has progressed markedly. She has put on a fair amount of weight, and I give her plenty of exercise to make sure it's all muscle. We'll go down to Steve's and go swimming this afternoon. It's all I can do to keep up with her when we're in the current.

99

The cat's OK. I still don't know her name, though. She sleeps all day, and I don't know what she does at night. I suppose she stays in the house, for she was raised as a house cat. She uses a litter box, but I want to teach her to go outside. At least the mice haven't been eating my rice since I got her.

The town is finally working on the house. They're rewiring the house, so I suppose I'll have electricity in a while. I really don't need electricity, though. I'd rather have a table and a closet for the kitchen and a closet for the bedroom. I hope they give me paint, too. That would be nice.

My social life is busier than my working life. I've played tennis with the Belgian doctors the past two nights in a row. I broke the strings in my racquet the first night, so I'll have to buy some heavy fish line in the marché and re-string the racquet myself. I hope to go back up to Lusanga and play bridge again soon. It's really enjoyable up there.

I guess I best sign off now, fish work to do. I pray that all is well. Take care and don't worry too much.

Love,
John

April 20, 1976

Dear Mom and Dad,

This is a French keyboard typewriter I'm using, so expect a few mistakes. The a, q, w, x, z, and m are mixed-up. Plus, you have to capitalize for periods and numbers.

I hope everybody had a nice Easter. Mine was rather unexciting; I slept most of the day as I'll explain later.

Last week I spent four days out in various villages seventy kilometers south of here. Merrill Ewart is a Mennonite missionary (American) who does agricultural extension work. I was doing a little fishery survey work while I was gone, but I spent most of the time with Merrill while he was doing his work. He is collecting information for his dissertation on rural teaching. The following is a condensation of the notes I took.

From April 13 to 18, I was with Merrill Ewart on an extension trip to seven bwalas (rural villages with ten to several hundred people, these averaged around fifty). He is asking people during a bwala meeting to describe their problems. These are some of the things they mentioned:

I. Work
    Since Belgians left and Zairians took over the factories (especially palm oil) things have fallen apart: no work; no trucks to haul produce; workers aren't paid for work done (managers keep all the money); taxes are very high; people (especially young) are forced into thievery due to lack of work

II. Hospitals and dispensaries
    None close by, are expensive, no medications, many people (especially little children) get sick and die (due more to their poor diet in my opinion), women forced to give birth on the ground

III. Store goods
    Aren't many goods in stores, everything is expensive, only saka-saka and luku to eat, there's no salt (approximately $50 for a twenty-five-kg sack)

IV. Crops
    Manioc is drying up; merchants don't come to buy our goods (manioc, soy beans, corn, peanuts); fields are far away and very large (due to government policy, poor soil condition, and poor agricultural practices); each

101

woman has to work a fifty-meter by fifty-meter plot (all the more land for the government to tax); no tools to work with; one can't raise fish because thieves will just steal them (they used to burn thieves, but now we have to put them in prison so they no longer have any fear of stealing); no more wild game since guns scared them all away

V. Personal observations and interesting remarks mentioned:

- When asked who'll die first if there is no food they laughed because it's obvious that the kids are the first to do without.
- Old men would challenge us (white people); you just talk, you say you are here to help us but you won't give us a ride in your Land Rover or give us work. You can easily give us work but why are you holding out on us?
- If you don't salt your food you get worms.
- (Old man) All this talk is nice, but you'll go away and we'll still have our problems.
- People feel God gave white men all the brains. "We have no intelligence." (A very sad sentiment.)
- A little kid once looked at his hand after I shook it, so I looked at mine—all the kids in the group thought this was hilarious.
- When we aren't in their presence, people call us sons of Saint Marie.
- Bwalas are 60% kids, 20% women (all those fifteen and up have kids, it seems at least half the woman are always nursing a child), 10% old men, and maybe 10% teenagers (young people leave the bwala and never come back).

- People think canned sardines give diarrhea, which is funny for I have been eating pilchards seven days a week.
- Women and children cluster, while men are separated. Men do most of the talking; only in two of the bwalas did the men give the women equal standing to speak. Many women won't speak in Kikongo, but in their own dialect.
- People are very poorly dressed: pants, shirts, and dresses are all very tattered and torn, very few people have shoes.
- They want us to come back with a decision for all their problems.
- Many men mentioned it's their problem (responsibility, rather) to take care of the child when they make a woman pregnant. "But how can we when there's no work, no money?"
- Anxiety mentioned about children leaving and never knowing their parents.
- Mentioned how well off they were during the Belgian reign; there was food, money, clothes, stores filled with goods; the people weren't poor they tell us.
- People were up in arms against merchants and government officials; bunch of thieves, nothing but bribes, taxes, poor prices for goods produced, expensively priced when resold.
- Almost all the goods we now produce rot on the side of the road.
- People have become lazy (not true in my opinion, though) for there is no work.
- Mondele (white people) are holding out, they can give us trucks and roads but aren't.

- Lot of sick people out there, they're thin and weak, many kids have cuts with flies buzzing around; polio, and TB are common.

Until the government and commerce systems are straightened up (coup d'état?) the people don't stand a chance out in the bush. There's a lot of hostility among the common people towards high Zairian officials, qu'est-ce qu'il y aura?

The people do tend to be lazy. They could at least work on their own subsistence level, agricultural practices (raise fish!). However, their gripes are legitimate and overwhelming.

I feel my job is important and it is definitely worth doing. But I certainly am frustrated trying to work with this country's inept agricultural bureaucracy. This is a rich, rich country. I only wish for the people's sake that it gets itself organized.

John

April 28, 1976

Dear Mom,

Your package arrived last week. Thanks for the curtains and seeds.

I haven't been too busy around here lately. Steve has been at a development meeting in Spain so I've been doing his job as regional representative: answer the radio, shuttle people to and from the airport, take care of the volunteers' medical problems.

I played bridge Friday, Saturday, and Sunday evening here in Kikwit. It was a lot of fun. Once I even made seven hearts but unfortunately only bid four. Last night I had dinner with three OxFam people, all British. They had a lot of fun with my American accent. It's also amazing how many different expressions each language has.

Tomorrow the director of OxFam from England will be here in Kikwit looking over some of their programs. He'll also drop by the fish station and either Steve (if he returns tomorrow morning) or I will give him a tour. It'll be rather difficult to be optimistic about the station development considering the lack of government involvement. It's a shame we're finding funds for the project but that there's a lack of responsibility among those for whom the station exists.

Sorry so short, but I have to go.

Love,
John

May 9, 1976

Dear Mom,

It's hard to believe it's May, school's almost/is over, summer's around the corner, and it has been a year since I left. Time really flies here, especially since all the months are the same. It's just as hot and humid now as it was in December.

The February issue of *Reader's Digest* arrived, along with a confirmation on the *National Wildlife* subscription. There was an interesting article mentioned in R.D. about Canada not giving foreign aide to countries whose government is not actively involved in their own country's development. That makes a lot of sense to me, for I know there's no way all the millions of dollars Kissinger is giving Mobutu will ever reach the poor people out here in the little villages. The people know that, too, that any money upper class Zairians have will not trickle down to them.

All last week I was in the same bwala I was in before. Kitabi

is its name. (I trust by now you've received my typed letter.) I gave eight Zairian extension agents a stage (training course) in fish culture. They work for the American-Canadian Mennonite Mission of Kikwit. They're a well-chosen bunch: intelligent, active, and interested in helping their people. During the morning we worked on building a dam to one pond, and in the afternoons I gave four, two-hour lectures on fish culture. This

is certainly the most important thing I've done since I've been here, for they will be here long after I leave and will be able to continue what I have started. I'll stick with them for the rest of my term and reinforce what I've already taught them.

How's Rose enjoying her first major haircut? It doesn't sound like she was upset as she was when her hair was trimmed a while ago.

Love,
John

May 18, 1976

Dear Mom and Dad,

Hello again, hope everyone's OK. Have you started making any plans for this summer yet? I'll be sticking around here most of the time. I may do some far-flung extension work up to two hundred kilometers away, though.

The Nzinda station is still in the doldrums. The commissioner of agriculture for the région has promised us three times now that Ngam would be assigned to our program. Steve and I have talked about it, and if no definite action is taken within this month we may/will totally abandon our attempts with a government fish station. In that case, I probably would move and work strictly with extension. Without full government cooperation, fishery development will be very slow. So, we feel that if they want a fish station, they'll have to at least give us a good, honest agronome.

I wish I could spend 100% of my time with the Nzinda project, for I realize the need and potential of a decent station here. Maybe the commissioner's promise will be fulfilled in the near future.

Dad, could you please deposit Aunt Bobbie's check into one of the accounts? It was a late Christmas present that came by boat.

The March *Reader's Digest* arrived today. I hope the wildlife magazines come OK. I enjoy reading those quite a bit. Do you have any news on Dr. Jansegers's *National Geographic* subscription? (If you didn't receive that letter, please order Dr. P. Jansegers, B.P. 188 Kikwit a one-year subscription to *N. G.* and use my money to pay for it.)

I'm pretty tired, have a little bit of a head cold, too, not bad, though. I think I'll hit the sack.

Love,
John

May 27, 1976

Dear Mom,

Mail seems to be slowing down at this end of the line. What used to take two weeks now takes four. I don't know why that is. I suppose mail service is falling as quickly as the economy.

The past week has been a busy one for me fish-wise. We harvested two ponds at Nzinda, and Steve hauled six hundred fingerlings and fifty breeders to three of the guys by boat. I am now starting to transport fish to my extension contacts.

I stocked one small pond in Kikwit, and then I hauled eighty fish in a fifty-five-gallon (200-liter) drum eighty kilometers to an agricultural research center. Yesterday, I transported one hundred fingerlings in two, twenty-liter plastic jugs 130 kilometers (four and one-half hours) to a Trappist mission. By doing it, I'm learning how to transport fish. I didn't know if the fish would survive in those little jugs, but not one died. However, I left the one hundred fish in a big steel tub outside overnight. Being at an elevation of eight hundred meters, it gets quite chilly at night. Since Tilapia are tropical fish, they aren't able to survive much cold, and thirteen fish died by the morning. At 6:15 I added two coffee pots of hot water that kept any more fish from dying. The fish arrived at the ponds a little stunned, but OK.

The work at Nzinda has been zero for quite some time now. It has almost been three months now and the government still hasn't hired Ngam—just promises, promises.

Working with extension is a much more rewarding experience than rebuilding a government station. I certainly am a lot happier now than I was three months ago before I did much work in the field.

I now have two chicken coops. The first is for egg production with ten hens. I now have five, three-month-old hens. I'm going to augment that to ten laying hens. The second coop is for broiler production. The coop is divided into three sections, so each month I'll buy ten, one-month-old chicks and each month I'll harvest ten, twelve-to-sixteen-week-old birds. That'll keep me in chicks and eggs, and I'll sell a lot, too.

Love,
John

June 8, 1976

Dear Mom, Dad, and everyone else,

Thanks for your letter of May 7. I received it yesterday. The former ten-to-fourteen-day mail delivery has changed to one month, too bad. I hope my letters are coming through.

I had another interesting weekend. One of the other fish volunteers had his first fish harvest. He stocked this two are (200 square meters: 20 m by 10 m) pond back in December. During the past six months, the farmer (Mamvaka) fed his fish daily with ground peanuts, rice bran, and termites. He also had a good plankton bloom and good compost piles in the pond. At any rate, he fed his fish as intensively as possible, and in this short pe-

riod of time he raised fifty-five kg of fish from two kilos of fingerlings. This is twice the production we thought farmers could produce. Needless to say we're quite excited about it. If this can't help us find more support for our project (especially from the Zaire government), nothing will.

Speaking of the government, if we don't receive a definite confirmation from Kinshasa of Ngam's placement in our program to run the Nzinda station by June 20, I'm changing sites. I'm doing a fair amount of work around the Kikwit area, but not as much as I could do as a full-time extension agent.

After the harvest Saturday, I went to Lusanga and visited a Belgian technician (Bert). We played two-and-one-half sets of tennis (he's excellent) (0–6; 4–6; 3–4) that afternoon, and he treated me to a fine dinner at his house with rosé wine. (Bourgeois, aren't we?) I stayed there Sunday, and that evening we played bridge with two Catholic pères and Bill Fiebig, another fish PCV. Between the five of us, we played four rubbers (five clubs was the best I could do). I enjoy playing bridge. It's funny I never really learned how to play at home.

Tomorrow I'll be leaving for Due where Bill will have his first harvest, so it should be another interesting weekend.

J'espère que tout le monde aura un bon été. (Ann, translate that!)

Love,
John

June 15, 1976

Dear Mom and Dad,

I've received eight letters this week. Mail service may be picking up again. Please send me an absentee ballot plus any registration material I may need. I'm not sure if P.C. Zaire will provide that or not. I'm receiving *National* and *International Wildlife* and *Reader's Digest* OK. I'm also able to read *International Newsweek* (usually two weeks old—not bad) and listen to VOA, BBC, and Voix de France. I'm never up-to-date but certainly close enough. Thanks for ordering *National Geographic* for the doc, Dad.

We had another harvest this past Saturday in Due (130 kilometers from Kikwit at Bill Fiebig's post). Six of us were out there to help Bill transport fingerlings to other farmers' ponds that were ready to be stocked. We would put fifty fish in a half-filled plastic bag (one-half water, one-half air). Then we'd take as many fish as we needed and put them in our backpacks and take off on our motorcycles. We moved around 1,000 fingerlings to seven or eight ponds up to twenty kilometers (thirty minutes) from the harvested pond. It was an interesting, full day's work.

That evening was a big night at the Due Bar. The group shared several cases of beer between a bunch of friends and us, and there was quite a bit of dancing as well. However, after all the day's activities, I was too burned out to stay up for the nightlife. By 9:00, I was ready to crash and went to sleep inside the Land Rover until we went back to the Catholic mission where we were staying.

We went back to Kikwit the next day and along the road we found a chameleon. It has a body length of six inches and its tail is around nine inches long. It's amazing how it changes colors, from solid green to brown, blue, yellow, black, and green spots and stripes. We brought it back to Kikwit, and Steve's keeping it as a pet force—feeding it moths.

Steve went to Kinshasa today to talk with several Zairian officials about bringing Ngam into our program. We've waited over three months now. If Steve receives no definite response this week, I will be leaving Kikwit, for I can do more fish work elsewhere. I'll let you know as soon as I do.

Love,
John

June 27, 1976

Dear Dad,

I'm sorry it has been so long since I sent any film home. The reason why is that we've used my camera for fishery purposes (PR) and had one roll developed in Kinshasa.

I hope you receive this film OK, Dad. Happy 51st birthday—sorry I'm not there for the cake. I really enjoy development work, though, frustrations and all. It's pretty tough to say how much time I'll spend at home the next few years. Maybe I'll learn Spanish and work in Latin America next. It's not so far away.

Love,
John

June 28, 1976

Dear Mom,

Your letters of the 3rd and 14th arrived OK. Thanks for Bob's picture. Things are still in a confused state here. I'm not sure what I'll be doing. Steve Anderson spent the last eleven days in Kinshasa to no avail. He spoke with many of the agricultural officials, but they don't seem to want to cooperate with our project. We want Ngam hired as the agronome for the Nzinda station. We know he's the best man for the job. However, there seems to be some personality conflicts in the upper echelons with Ngam. Various funding organizations (such as A.I.D., OxFam, Tilapia International) have offered to support us—even pay Ngam's salary. It's amazing and sad how much politics can interfere with development.

We're 90% sure Ngam won't be hired, so we'll totally abandon the station until we receive the cooperation we require. This Wednesday, Steve, the P.C. Zaire ag. director (Karl), and I will drive out to Idiofa to check a development project (privately funded and operated) out there. They have asked Steve for a fish culture volunteer. We're ahead of their schedule, but I hope they'll still be able to take me.

I've only written around four letters this month, one to Karen and the rest home. I feel like I've abandoned some of my friends—hope things get settled this week.

I'm sending two rolls of film home this week. One has already been developed. (A volunteer will mail it from New York around the 20th.) We used some of the shots of the developed roll for public relations in Kinshasa. It took them three months to return a set of slides to me, though, so I'm not going to give them the second roll. However, please make slide copies of fishery-related pictures and send them back to me. I'm hoping the package will arrive before Dad's birthday, but if not, Happy Birthday anyway.

If work were progressing well, Kikwit would be a nice place to live. There's a good European-American community. We're even organizing a tennis club. I've worked on my yard for over eight months now and am obtaining some produce from it. It's just a shame things aren't ideal politically.

I know I said this last time, but I'll say it again—maybe in my next letter I'll be able to tell you what I'll be doing soon.

Love,
John

July 5, 1976

Dear Mom and Dad,

Thanks for your letter of June 7, Dad. If I hear of any of my friends who may be able to use some of your assistance I'll let them know of your new insurance profession. I'm glad to hear your venture is starting out well.

I had an interesting trip out to Idiofa this past week. It looks like I'll be moving out there before long. There is a Belgian development organization (Progrès Populaire) centered in Idiofa with three other centers situated in the Zone. We visited Idiofa and the center 130 kilometers north of Idiofa (Mbeo). I'll return by myself tomorrow to better look at all four sites and choose the one where I want to work. I suppose I'll move within three weeks.

This is quite an organization, doing crop production and animal husbandry research, demonstration, and rural education. They certainly are providing a part of the infrastructure needed to the people of the Zone of Idiofa. It certainly will be a far more satisfying experience for me working for them than trying to get some action out of a disinterested government.

I suppose you folks celebrated the 4th with quite a bit of gusto. Yesterday morning we were on the road back from

Idiofa, and it wasn't until 10:00 AM before we remembered it was the 4th of July, 1976. We didn't celebrate the 4th in any way—just had a quiet dinner at the hotel (steak, French fries, and beer—the menu never changes).

This is it for now. Hope all's well.

Love,
John

July 13, 1976

Dear Mom and Dad,

Happy Birthday, Dad. I hope things continue well for you. Have you decided when you'll retire from government service and go into money management full swing? Mom, received your June 23 and July 2 letters. Sounds like everyone's fairly active back there. Hope Sue's and Ann's cuts are healing up OK.

I've been in Idiofa for the past week, just returned yesterday (140 kilometers of dusty, bumpy, sand-trapped roads—three-and-one-half hours). Things look real good there. I'll be moving out when Steve gets back (left today for Kinshasa) towards the end of July. I'm really excited about it. Idiofa's a nice town (10–20,000). I'll be working with the Dévelopement Progrès Populaire. It's a very active organization sponsored by a Catholic mission that provides the infrastructure needed to help improve the agricultural practices of the people. I'll be in charge of the fisheries development in that area, with about a thirty-kilometer radius (I hope). There's a lot of fishery

117

potential out there and a lot of enthusiasm. I know I'll enjoy living there, may even spend an extra year or two.

When I came back yesterday, I was fortunate enough to catch Steve before he left for Kinshasa and then the U.S. I told him he had to drop by for a visit. I should have written this letter last night so he could have delivered it himself. By the time you read this, he'll have returned.

I had my tennis racquet restrung in Kinshasa. They did not have a good quality nylon string, so I had gut put in (21.50 z). I'm worried that the humidity may ruin it, but it's all I could get. I've never seen a racquet strung so tightly. They're certainly quality strings.

My cat walked off one night around a month ago and has never come back. I don't know if she'd be able to take care of herself. I don't believe Siamese cats are usually too bright. Boogie's doing fine, except for the fact that I've been gone all month and am leaving tomorrow for a week in Masi-Manimba. She stays at another PCV's house and does OK.

Love to all,
John

P.S. Tell Tom Happy Birthday. I'll write him a letter, but it'll be late.

July 19, 1976

Hello Tom,

If we're lucky, you'll get this by the 2nd, if not, Happy 19th anyway. In just another short year, you'll join the ranks of us "old men." I've heard you're working for the Bureau of

Mines, U. of MD. What type of work are you doing? Today I wrote Mom and Dad, too, and I spoke about a conversation I had with a père. The day before that he took me to one of his swimming holes. It was a beautiful spot. The river was around twenty-meters wide in a U-shaped bend. The water was crystal clear with a very sweet taste; palm trees, vines, and jungle surrounded us. It was here that he told me we're better off than millionaires. We have pure water, clean air, no noise, and a very congenial populace. Many people in developed countries pity the poor African in his mud house, but I am now starting to wonder if it is not we who should be pitied. One nice thing about this job, you sure do get to see the other side of the coin. It's nice what we have back in the States, but it's good to realize much of it isn't necessary.

Now that Jim has bought a motorcycle, are you thinking of getting a license to drive it? If you do, I'm sure you'll enjoy it; I'd take a bike before a car any day. However, you have to drive a bike 100% defensively. One mistake and that's that.

I guess this is it for now. Have a nice summer and good luck in school next year.

Take care,
John

July 19, 1976

Dear Mom and Dad,

I just came back from a trip to Kingunji, a Catholic mission 160 kilometers west of here. They asked me to judge

119

the feasibility of creating a three-hectare (six-acre) lake in the valley eighty kilometers south of Kingunji. It certainly was a beautiful valley. A four-meter-high by forty-meter-long dam would have created a large lake. However, now during the middle of the dry season there are a thousand liters of water per second passing through the valley. Who knows how much during the rainy season? Such a large flow of water requires a fairly fancy diversion and spillway system, far more than the mission wanted to tackle. It would have cost a good $5,000, so they decided to let it go.

I spent some time with the Père Supérieur there. He's an interesting person, speaks English fairly well, too. The day before yesterday we walked to the top of a hill overlooking the mission and several villages, a beautiful site. Up there we talked a little about the people's culture, that to a European or an American, the African villager could seem very backwards and stupid. Sadly enough, he said that he has known Europeans who've lived twenty-five years in the Congo who never even tried to find out what these people are actually like. I certainly enjoy being able to sit down in a little village and talk with the people, learn about their ways of life, what they want their children to do and become, etc. Raising fish is only one aspect of the many things I enjoy experiencing here.

This is another reason why I'll be glad to move to Idiofa, for I'll be in much closer contact with the village people. Kikwit is a city with a large white population, and the Zairians are a mixture of people from all over, especially students from Kinshasa. At any rate, it is not an authentic African situation, and I feel it hurts my rapport with the Zairian villagers being a Kikwit "mondele" (white man).

All's fine here. I hope Steve had time to drop by. I trust all are well (stitches out?).

Love,
John

July 19, 1976

Hello Susan,

How is your hand? Mom told me you fell down in the woods and had to have stitches put in your palm. You even watched the doctors put them in, didn't you?

Thank you for your letter. It was very nice. I found "I love you" in your house. You're very smart to think of a game like that.

The weather in Zaire is much different than in Maryland. Right now it is the dry season, and it doesn't rain. The next time it will rain will be September. The mornings are a little chilly, but by ten to eleven o'clock it is very warm. It does not get real hot like Maryland, though.

You must be getting very tall if you can kneel in the big pool. If you keep trying, you will be able to swim before long. Are you afraid to put your head under water?

What trips have you gone on this summer? Mom told me about your trip to King's Dominion. Have you made any more trips?

You drew me a nice house, so I'll draw you another house. This is called a pyote (pie-ote). It is just used to sit in, chat, and drink palm wine. The roof is grass and the sides are all sticks. Even on a

very hot day it is cool inside the pyote. The grass keeps the sun out, and the wind blows through the walls. It is very nice.

Everyone is all right here. I hope everyone is OK there, too.

I love you, Sue.

Your brother,
John

July 29, 1976

Hi Bobby,

How have you been this summer? Mom told me you just had your swimming test. Was it difficult? How did you do? It took me a long time to learn how to swim. I think I was nine years old before I could swim across the pool. What skills are you now doing?

I just watched a small lizard catch and eat a fly. The fly was trapped in a window and the lizard chased him until the fly tired and slowed down. Then with one last lunge the lizard opened his mouth, shot out his tongue, and grabbed the doomed fly. I suppose it tasted quite good.

Hopefully, you will receive this before your birthday so that my "Happy Birthday, Big Bob!" isn't late. It doesn't seem too long ago when I wrote to you for your seventh birthday, and now you're already eight. You will graduate from high school before you know it! I'll bring you a present when I finally come home.

Have you ever gone fishing with Jim this year? Ask him to take you fishing for your birthday so that you can catch some big blue fish.

I guess this is all for now, good luck in third grade.

Love, your big brother in Africa,
John

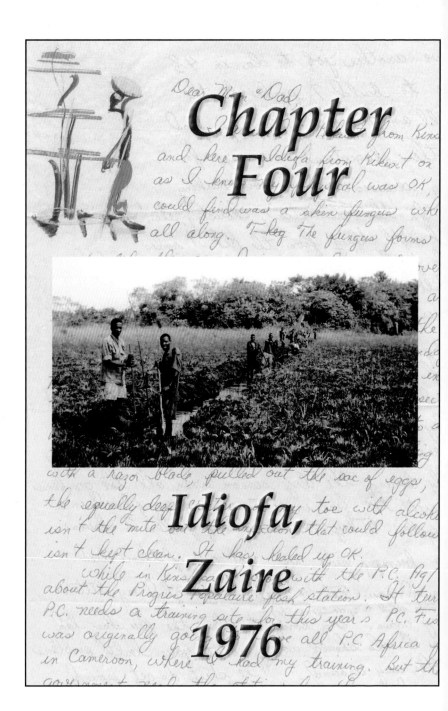

Chapter Four

Idiofa, Zaire 1976

August 26, 1976

Dear Mom and Dad,

I'm sorry my letters are rather sporadic right now. I hope to ameliorate that as I settle in.

The dry season has ended early this year (usually mid-September). We had a good storm yesterday, at least five bolts of lightning struck within 100 meters of the guesthouse I'm staying in. I have been told the storms will become far worse.

My fisheries program is starting to take shape. I plan to work intensively with five to eight farmers located around Idiofa and to use their work to teach other farmers around them. With Progrès Populaire I hope to build a small fish station where we'll have good fingerling production as well as demonstration and practice ponds. The one pond where I put some Tilapia on Aug. 5 already has some nests in it. I'll have fingerlings by late November.

Right now Progrès Populaire is building one six-meter dam to produce hydroelectric power. This one will produce

125

around 100 kilowatts, which will be used for an ag school complex they're building. In the future they plan on building a second dam, and they'd like me to survey the site. I'll have to measure the drop from the dam level to the base of the falls. There are around four cubic meters of water passing per second, and if that falls fifteen meters, that equals around 750 horsepower.

Boogie's found a lot of new friends already. A Frenchman (he's on vacation so I haven't met him yet) who works for Progrès Populaire has a nice male dog, and I may mate them. She's putting on weight, too. I'd guess she's more than sixty pounds.

We had another fisheries meeting in Bulungu last weekend. A man from U.S.A.I.D. and one from the American embassy attended. (Hopefully we'll get some funds for motorcycle maintenance.) More and more people are learning about our program, and I believe it'll turn into something quite exciting someday. Steve has already been asked to possibly be the director of fisheries for Peace Corps/West Africa. This could be a good steppingstone for all of us.

The airplane arrives today at 9:00 AM, so I must get this in the pouch quickly.

Love,
John

September 5, 1976

Dear Mom,

I received your Aug. 6 letter yesterday. The Idiofa address is not a good one as it turned out. I have yet to receive any mail through the Kinshasa address, but hopefully that will be quicker. The weekly plane to and from Kinshasa usually arrives on Wednesdays. Now that I'm getting settled in, I'll try to get my letters out once a week again.

Right now I'm staying in a room at the P.P. guesthouse. When the French administrator returns from vacation I may move in with him. The houses are small and functional: three bedrooms, one bathroom, and one living room-dining room. They're made of cement block and tin roofs. There's running water (usually all the time) and lights from 6:00 P.M. to 8:30 P.M.

I brought Boogie with me. She's doing quite well and has a lot of new friends already. I sold my chickens to a friend in Kikwit. The hens are now laying.

One excellent fact about Idiofa is that there are very few mosquitoes. On top of the plateau there is usually a good breeze, which keeps the mosquitoes down in the valleys.

Living among so many poor people puts one in a situation

that doesn't usually exist back home. I am often reminded about the biblical passages on the rich and the poor, for I am now certainly the rich man with many servants all around. I've seen the poor widow put one penny in the collection, which was all she had, while I can put in $10 and never miss it. Half-starved beggars come to your door asking for ten cents to buy a couple bananas. So you give them fifty cents, and they go away, just to be back in a few days. It's an unsettling position for me to live in, yet I know with proper management this country would have more than enough to provide for itself. Maybe it'll happen in my lifetime, though I doubt it.

I do believe I've found an excellent career in ag. development. I suppose I'll stick with it one way or another. I must say it has changed the pace of my life. Instead of completing things in a few months like a school term, it takes years to see much progress. So you do things little by little and hope something takes hold.

Thank Rose for her note. She types quite well.

Love,
John

September 15, 1976

Dear Mom and Dad,

Hello, all's coming along fine here. I trust everyone's good and busy back in school now. I received the letter with Bob's and Sue's additions; Sue certainly writes quite well for just starting second grade.

We have now completed two fingerling production ponds for P.P. This week or early next, I'll stock each with about forty fish. We'll build two or more fingerling ponds and then start building larger production ponds. There's enough land to dig up to four acres of ponds with a potential yearly production of eight tons of fish (That would be nice to see).

As soon as we have enough fingerlings, my main efforts will no longer be with the P.P. fish project, but with various farmers in the surrounding villages. Four people have already asked for advice, and that number will quickly increase as word is spread.

This week I visited one farmer. It's a beautiful twenty-eight-kilometer drive through several villages and through a fair amount of forest on footpaths. From his house, it's a four kilometer walk down to his pond. He has a poor site in that it's rather marshy. But, he's interested and a hard worker, so I think he'll be able to build three fair ponds. I worked up a good sweat walking back up the long hill to his house. The villages are up on the crest, for the wind keeps the mosquitoes and humidity down.

It's a great experience to sit with various villagers and chat while drinking palm wine. Before I left, we had lunch, luku and caterpillars (rubbery but OK). It's interesting that the people find a third to half of their animal protein in insects: caterpillars, grubs, crickets (big ones), termites, and I don't know what else.

The older people seem to have an adequate diet, but there are a lot of children who suffer from protein deficiency. The child is the first to do without, and their development is amazingly slow. A ten-year-old kid is about the size of a seven-year-old like Bob. (That is, as Bob was when I left.)

To finish my original story, after lunch the farmer gave me a bunch of bananas, which I tied to the motorcycle. The village people are very friendly and generous, and I feel far more accepted by them than by many city people. As my extension work picks up, I will become very content. This is what I came here to do, which I could not do in Kikwit.

Love to all,
John

September 22, 1976

Dear Everybody,

Mail has turned out to be excellent here in Idiofa—one week from the States. If you mail a letter by Tuesday or Wednesday, I'll receive it the following Wednesday. This past week Mom's Aug. 31, Sept. 8 and 14 letters arrived; thanks for the *Washington Post* clipping. Thank you, Sue, for your letter and picture. You're quite an artist.

We have now completed three fingerling ponds for the Progrès Populaire. I am now trying to recapture some of the brooders I stocked in another pond last month in order to stock these new ponds. It's an interesting method how we capture the fish. The fish are fed rice bran and termites daily each morning in the same area of the pond. They come as soon as you put the food in the water. So by laying a net under the feeding area, you bait the fish and lift the net while they are feeding. The first try we caught only eleven of 150 fish in the pond—the fish were wise to us. But other fish guys have caught 200 to 300 fingerlings at a pull with this system, so it's certainly efficient.

The compost is there to produce the phytoplankton that the fish feed on. Since the fish congregate in this area, too, I'll try to bait-trap them there tomorrow. I want to catch

100 of the 150 fish and divide them among four other fingerling ponds.

Some of the fish have already reproduced. So in two months we'll start selling fingerlings to farmers. All of the fingerling ponds should be in full production in four to five months, providing us with a steady supply of fingerlings. My days will become more and more busy as time goes by.

We're back in the rainy season now; however, the rains won't start in earnest for another month. The rains that we have had have cleared the sky a little (from the smoke of bush fires). Last night the stars were absolutely brilliant with the Milky Way splashed across the zenith. Orion has done its *tour du monde* and now returns to the midnight sky.

Best wishes to everyone.

Love,
John

Note: In October 1976, I made a surprise trip home for my parents' twenty-fifth wedding anniversary.

November 9, 1976

Dear Mom and Dad,

I'm still in Kinshasa and hope to go by Land Rover to Kikwit tomorrow. My flight was OK. We flew over the Sahara on Friday. That is desolate country. I sat next to a man from Louisiana who's working on the offshore oilrigs off Zaire, Cabinda, and Angola. It was interesting talking about his work. I'd like to see the ocean here sometime.

Zaire is still having a lot of economic problems. Fuel is supposed to become very scarce. I've heard that all electricity may be shut off in Kikwit if the situation doesn't improve in a month. Zaire has to import all refined petroleum products, and because it (Zaire) hasn't been repaying its loans no one will sell them any more fuel.

I'm afraid I've heard more bad news than good news in the short time I've been back. Steve Anderson may leave the fish program shortly. He has been having a lot of conflicts with the P.C. director over expanding the fish program. I'll be glad to talk with Steve and see what's going to happen.

Art Locke, one of the fish guys, has had recurring malaria, and if he has one more attack he'll have to go home. He's allergic to our main anti-malaria medicine, so he has to take a weaker drug that isn't doing the job. He's the guy for whom I brought the softball stuff.

It feels great to be back here, to be using French and Kikongo again. It'll be good to get back to work in Idiofa. I think I'm going to have a few fishery problems, though. I've heard some of my fish in one pond were dying. I'll let you know what I find.

Since there's not much news I'll sign off. Take care of yourselves, and I hope you have a nice Thanksgiving.

Love,
John

November 15, 1976

Dear Mom, Dad, and everybody,

I'm finally back in Idiofa. I had quite a trip from Kinshasa to Kikwit—twenty-eight hours for 300 miles. Three of us, two Zairian P.C. drivers going out to buy manioc, and I were in a P.C. Land Rover.

The road from Kinshasa to Kikwit is asphalted except for a fifty-mile stretch about two-thirds the way along. Unfortunately, the other guys didn't know the road too well and we took the old road to Kikwit—one hundred miles of washed-out dirt roads. The other two did not have much dirt-road experience and since the roads were so bad I drove in the dirt. We were following the signs to Kikwit as we went down this one hill with a tremendous washout down the middle. There was just enough room to squeeze the Land Rover between the embankment and the three-foot-deep gully. When the gully cut across the road I had to drop down into it (you'd be amazed what a L.R. can do—how far it can tip without falling over) and climb up the other side; this is all being done at night. So we started back down the good road, when not one hundred yards away, we saw the whole road gone. We had to turn around and climb back up through the mess we just came down.

Going up a rough spot is a lot harder than going down, and it's all the worse at night. I went into the gully and started climbing the steep side, but the rear wheels dug themselves into the sand right up to the axles.

I decided that was it, no way to dig out until morning, though we were only thirty miles from Kikwit. We slept in the vehicle, which was tilted way over on the left side with the nose sticking up in the air. The whole night, whenever I dozed off, I dreamed of a crane just happening to pull us out. I didn't think we could get out.

Light came at 5:15 and we acquired two worn-out shovels at the local village. With forty-five minutes of praying, shoveling, a little sweat, and two stiff boards, we were able to dig ourselves out and climb the hill. I was surprised we did it. It still took us until ten o'clock, though, to go the last thirty miles to Kikwit. It was rough enough in daylight, I'm glad I didn't have to do it at night.

My fish in one pond have done well and reproduced very heavily. However, of twenty-five fish I put in a second pond, twenty died. Why, I don't know. At any rate I have a lot of work ahead of me and am looking forward to seeing what I can do.

Jim, please bring books, dried pepper plants, and the Boy Scout knapsack in my closet (the little one).

Plane service to Idiofa is no longer regular, so I don't know what mail service will be like. My address will remain the same, though.

Love,
John

November 29, 1976

Dear Mom and Dad,

I received four letters this past week, from Sue and Bob, and Mom's Nov. 4 and 12. Mail service will be in the two-to-three-week range; there is no longer weekly air service to Idiofa.

Last weekend the fisheries team held its bimonthly meeting. We camped for three days, 180 kilometers south of Kikwit on the rim of a huge gorge. The gorge is actually a huge,

washed-out gully four hundred feet deep with the main river canyon and a series of box canyons. From the rim where we slept under the stars, the hill fell all the way to the base at a 45° angle, at least. There were a lot of interesting cliffs and mesa formations.

We had our first grand experience with African wildlife; several troops of baboons were in the various gorges. Four of us spent a whole day walking through several gorges. We were lost once. As we walked along the streams, from time to time we'd sink up to our knees in quicksand. All along the banks, there were hundreds of baboon tracks. We even saw the tracks of a cat, which we figured was the size of a puma.

We'd climb up and sit on the edge of a low cliff and wait for the baboons to come out. They're very curious, fearless animals (up to 100 pounds!), and they'd slowly come out to see who the strangers were. The closest that one baboon came to us was fifty yards, but around fifty of them put on a spectacular, acrobatic show along a cliff one hundred yards from our hilltop perch. They would run across sheer cliffs, holding onto ledges that were only inches wide. Some ledges even broke as they

135

ran over them, but no baboon ever fell. A ledge broke on one little baboon when he arrived in a spot where he couldn't go any farther. So he sat down for a few minutes to look the situation over. Finally he jumped up and over about five yards to another ledge and got out from there.

We even held conversations with a couple of them. One of them would bark at us, so we'd bark back at him. Then we'd wave our arms in the air, and he'd pound the ground a few times. It was great; we even saw mamas preening their babies. I took some good pictures, but a 200 mm telephoto lens would have been outstanding.

Mom, I haven't used the tablecloth yet because Noll is in Germany on vacation. I'm now eating with a French-Polish Communist (interesting).

Dad, please reorder the *P.F. Culturist* magazine for me. They've been sending me 1975 issues. Please ask them to send current issues. Don't bother changing addresses.

Love to all,
John

December 9, 1976

Dear Everybody,

I'm sorry I'm not writing once a week. I'm doing a lot of fishery extension work. I'll try to keep it at least once every ten days, *assez régulièrement*.

I just finished a six-day, six-hundred-kilometer extension tour. And on rutted, dirt roads driving a little 100cc motorcycle, that's a long way. I was reminded of my cross-country trips back home.

People all over Idiofa Zone, mostly Catholic missions, are asking for fish advice. I hope to see as many as I can, but I'll only work with the most progressive people; I haven't enough time for everyone.

My trip started out roughly. I wasn't thirty minutes outside of Idiofa heading north when the sky opened up. I had used my raincoat to wrap up my baggage, and, quite stupidly, I left my nylon jacket in Idiofa. So I stopped and stood under a tree, getting soaked and freezing for two hours. It was in the middle of nowhere, not a village, nothing, up on top of the savanna. It was actually very beautiful watching the rain come down and thinking how warm and dry we usually stay. I was slightly scared, though, by lightning less than a mile away, I know I shouldn't sit under a lone tree during a storm, but I would have frozen to death if I sat under a cloud.

The rain slacked off a bit, so I went on for two or three kilometers, and the downpour returned. So I hid myself again. This continued a couple more times before I arrived at a village (enfin!). I stayed in a nice hut for an hour while the rain cleared. The moma there fed me some hot luku and a fine sauce with more caterpillars, and to top it off there were some juicy crickets. Good chop; warmed me up.

It was now 4:00 PM, and I still had sixty km to go if I continued to my original destination. No way. Ngosso, another Catholic mission with two PCVs, was only fourteen km away. So, I holed up there for the night. Soeur Stella (a talkative Italian) took good care of me. She prepared a huge bed with a thick mattress and a warm blanket. It's amazing how a cold, wet dog could wind up in such a warm nest in just a few hours.

I'm cleaning up and landscaping my yard now. It was overgrown with grass and weeds two feet tall. We don't have lawn mowers (I think I mentioned this before), so I earned some more blisters with my coup-coup. I've already planted some cactus (I'll never see the fruits of my work) and will plant some bananas, papayas, frangi pangi, poinsettia, a garden, and flowers. I would like to raise rabbits, but I'll be away from the house too often to care for them. Maybe I'll do it anyway.

Rosie, thanks for your letter. I hope you received a good report card.

Mom, if you're not doing it already, could you please save my letters? They're a better journal than what I keep here.

Merry Christmas.

Bonnes vacances!
John

December 19, 1976

Dear Mom,

I hope everyone had an enjoyable Christmas. Happy Birthday, too.

Steve and I drove in to Kinshasa today. He's on his way home, for his P.C. contract has ended. He plans on being back in Kikwit in six weeks, though, working on a manioc improvement project for another organization. Meanwhile, we don't know what the future of our fisheries program is.

Jim, Les, and Mary will arrive the day after tomorrow; they'll be surprised to see me here in Kinshasa. Their vacation here will be very interesting both for them and me.

A week ago, I went 120 kilometers north of Idiofa to Mangai on the Kasai River. There's a Zairian priest at the mission there who is starting to do some ag. work and has a group of farmers interested in fish culture. I saw their ponds, which are in an excellent site and can be easily improved. We then had a two-hour class where I explained intensive fish culture to them and how they can rearrange their valley to suit it. These farmers were industrious in their work, and they seemed receptive to my new ideas. So, I intend to return there shortly and see how they're following my advice. I think it'll be a good place to work, though a bit far away.

I had another interesting trip just yesterday on my way to Kikwit from Idiofa. I wanted to leave Idiofa at 2:00 PM on my motorcycle to arrive before nightfall at 6:00. At 2:00, though, the sky opened up. I decided I had best go anyway for otherwise it would get dark. So I donned my nylon jacket, rubber pants, and rubber boots and was off. However, I hadn't gone two kilometers when three bolts of lightning crashed too close to me for comfort. I returned home and sat out the storm until 3:30.

By that time, the rain had tapered off enough that I could leave, but it still drizzled on me for two hours. The road was terrible, puddles everywhere and mud holes up to a foot deep. The bike slipped out from under me once (going ten mph down a sloped embankment), and I had to strong-arm and stiff-leg her quite often to keep her upright. The eighty-five-mile trip normally takes three-and-one-half hours, but I took five, arriving at 8:30 at night without a quarter cup of gas to spare. I sure was lucky, for if I had broken down, I would have been lost without a flashlight on a moonless evening. It was a beautiful ride in a way, though.

We left Kikwit at 5:40 this morning and rolled into Kinshasa at 4:00 P.M., not bad for three hundred miles. There is a paved road, but it's half worn away—no maintenance. At least we didn't have a thirty-hour trip as when I went from Kinshasa to Kikwit.

Love to all and Meilleurs Voeux
for the New Year,
John

Chapter Five

Idiofa, Zaire 1977

January 17, 1977

Dear Mom and Dad,

I hope I haven't gained any enemies since I haven't written in over a month. While Jim, Mary, and Leslie were here, I wasn't able to sit down long enough to write—too exuberant to discipline myself. At any rate, with their stories and pictures, you should be up to date.

It was a great experience for me to have a group of close friends over. To explain my situation here in Zaire to everyone at home, even with slides, is very difficult. But now that Jim and the girls have gone the route, they'll be able to comprehend far better what I'm doing over here. Seeing my job through their eyes was very rewarding for me.

My work is coming along great. I have seven ponds stocked with fish, and five more are ready to be stocked. Jim and the girls saw one of my extension sites at Banga-Banga (with the priest who spoke English). In just the week after we were there, the farmers followed my advice precisely and now have excellent ponds ready to be stocked. I believe that in this one site they'll construct over twenty ponds with a total water surface area of over one acre, enough for a potential production of 5,000 pounds of fish per year. It's a fabulous morale booster to work with this group of farmers. I always have a warm welcome when I arrive. They're a truly hard-working lot. They always say how pleased they are to have me direct their efforts, and I can't leave without coming into someone's house for a little food and drink. Experiences such as this make any inconveniences I have here seem paltry.

I hope you had an enjoyable Christmas back home. We certainly had an excellent one here. Please extend my thanks to Jerry and Bob for their presents. I'll write them shortly. Thank you for the shirts; they're excellent for the weather in Idiofa.

Brother Jim and friends Mary and Leslie visit from the USA.

Postage has gone sky-high in Zaire, from 17k to 91k, so I'm told. At the present official exchange rate, that's $1.00 a letter. The paper and envelope are five cents. This may aggravate my already lax writing habits, but I'll keep trying to be regular.

Love to all,
John

February 1, 1977

Dear Mom and Dad,

I just returned today from another tour, this one to the south. Two missions down there have asked about fish. Eighty miles is too far away for me to check up regularly on the farmers' work, but if I can teach the two Belgian priests enough about fish culture, they can direct the farmers. I'm getting so much work now I have to decide how best to divide up my time.

Thanks for your letters. They pour in three to my one. I do write two or three letters a week as an average; there sure are a lot of people to whom I like to write. You mentioned Ann's graduation photo in one letter; however, it wasn't enclosed. Please send me one if there are any left.

You asked me about my plans for the future. Well, they're nebulous at best. I am extending here for a third year. I truly believe that the Lord has dropped an excellent job in my lap, and I shouldn't leave it too hastily. If I don't feel I've finished after three years I may stay for a fourth, it's hard to say. I suppose I'll finish here in November 1978. Peace Corps will pay for a one-month vacation. I have yet to decide when to take it, though. Graduate school in fisheries science is in the back of my mind, though that's too far ahead to be sure about.

It is sad being away from the family, not seeing the little ones growing up. The hardest day in my life was watching Jim walk back to the plane in Kinshasa. But we all have our responsibilities in life. God, through both of you, has blessed me with a life where I never had to suffer. It's my job to return that favor to others, and I'm trying to learn here how to do it. I won't be here forever, for my home is on the east coast. There's a lot of work to do there. But I want to leave here knowing that I've done a good job and grown a little in the process.

Let me close by quoting Jim in his letter that he wrote as he flew out of Kinshasa:

> "One thing that really dominated my thinking was knowing, and for the first time actually understanding what poverty is, and to think that Dad grew up under the same conditions of despair for a few years of his youth. But he has worked so hard to insure that we, the family, shall never experience the hardships that he endured. I am grateful for Mom's and Dad's unselfishness. How truly lucky we are."

Thanks, Mom and Dad.
Your son, John

February 9, 1977

Dear Everybody back home,

How's the winter coming along? I hear a lot of grim news on the radio about 0° weather for weeks on end in the northeast and natural gas running low.

I could have used some of that cold weather here. Today I walked over five miles looking at five village pond sites. I'm sure I lost a couple quarts of sweat, walking up and down several steep hills under a hazy tropical sun.

I think I already mentioned that Progrès Populaire is planning on expanding their fish station to a dozen or so ponds covering three to four acres. This afternoon I started placing the stakes to survey the whole plain. This will certainly be my largest single project. They're investing a fair amount of money into this, so I hope it produces fish. My calendar is already filled to March between this and my village projects.

On Monday and Tuesday we built a rack for my motorcycle to carry gasoline and fish. The rack is solid enough, but I don't think the motorcycle could take more than forty to fifty pounds of luggage. The weight is set too far behind the rear axle and that causes the rear tire to bottom into the fender whenever I hit a bad bump.

While Jim was over, he met Patrick, the vet for P.P. He was in this weekend from his post, and we were talking together one evening at the hotel. He and his fiancée would like to come and visit parts of America for a couple months. So we thought of possibly going on a motorcycle trip together when I finish here. I think it would be quite an experience for them and me. Pat wants to go into Mexico and Canada, too. We'd have to be in Nebraska for the harvest, probably in 1979. If I go to grad school in September that would work out OK. He'll be thirty-one then, and he figures he'll have too many responsibilities to take an extended trip later on, plus having someone who knows people across the country would make the trip far more meaningful. I was surprised when he told me he's twenty-nine; he doesn't look any older than I.

I guess this is all for now. Hope all are well.

Take care,
John

February 17, 1977

Dear Mom and Dad,

Letters are coming in quite regularly at ten days to two weeks. I hope mine are coming in quickly enough. I'm in luck, though, because P.C. volunteers can now mail letters by the diplomatic pouch. This would make my mail nearly certain to arrive in one to two weeks. However, I need thirteen-cent stamps mailed to me from the States. So please send me around $5 worth the next time you write. If I ever go to Kinshasa, I'll see if I can buy some stamps from Americans I know there.

This past week I surveyed the marshy plain where the Progrès Populaire is building its pond series. I made a grid by placing stakes every twenty-five meters at right angles. I then took the levels of all these points (about 120) with a transit and plotted everything on graph paper. The plain is 400 m long by 200 m wide, and, according to my plan, we can build eight ponds of 0.8 hectares each (two acres) and fifteen smaller ponds of 0.04 hectares each. Seeing how there are no others, this has the potential of being the best fish station in Zaire. I hope P.P. decides to go ahead and build it.

My farmers keep me busy running around, too. Tomorrow I'm leaving on a three-day tour of 300-plus kilometers to see six extension contacts. Today I tried to catch some fingerlings for a village cooperative south of here. We dragged the net across the pond, and I know we had a lot of fish caught. However, we hit a palm stump that I didn't know was there, and all but ten fish got away while the net was hung up. Not only that, but a slimy leech latched onto me. They sure aren't any fun, for you bleed for ten to twenty minutes after you pull them off. And then, to top it off, I ripped my net on a split plank while cleaning it. Rough day fishing.

I'm also keeping myself busy editing a fish culture booklet in French and Kikongo, illustrated with original sketches. I wrote the original French copy; a père here revised it, improving my horrendous French; and someone else translated it into Kikongo. I have now slightly revised the French and Kikongo copies and am now typing the final draft. I'll then let the other fish guys go over it and revise it as they see fit. As soon as all is OK, OxFam (private British funding organization) has agreed to publish it. I suppose it'll be around twenty pages long.

So, it looks like I'm getting myself a little overextended, too. But it's far better than sitting around like I did for so long in Kikwit.

I trust all are well at home. Watch out for frostbite.

Love,
John

February 23, 1977

Dear Mom,

I just received your Feb. 7 letter; it sounds like mail service Zaire to U.S.A. is slowing up. I wrote on Jan. 17 and Feb. 1. I hope by now my letters are coming in. In my last letter, I explained the PCVs can now use the diplomatic pouch to mail letters and to send me $5 worth of 13-cent stamps. The mail arrives either in N.Y. or D.C. and from there goes overland.

I'm doing fine. My health is great, still haven't had so much as a queasy stomach. I may have lost a few pounds after coming back, but that's only because I gained them while at home. I'm eating very well, as Jim may have told you, but I run around too much to weigh more than my normal 140–145 pounds. No problem.

I just listened to President Carter's news conference on VOA. I have high hopes for his presidency. It seems he's concerned about problems facing common folk as well as the nation as a whole. He has changed priorities for U.S.A.I.D. grants. In the past, A.I.D. has spent money purely as a political lever, but now money cannot be committed unless the project can be proven to benefit the village people. I'm seeing millions of dollars spent overseas, and I'd like to know that they are both altruistically and efficiently spent. The weekend before last, I gave two A.I.D. team members a tour of a local village. They were studying the sale of grain to private and Zairian governmental buyers. I acted as the translator, English and Kikongo. It was quite interesting for all of us.

I've decided not to wait until next spring, but to come home for my mid-service vacation next Christmas. I've missed two already, so I think I ought to make it this year. If Jean (Frenchman here) decides to visit the U.S., he'll have to wait until the end of my tour here.

I don't really have much news; I wrote home less than a week ago plus to Sue and Rose the day before yesterday. There will be some news shortly on the fish station, though. I'll keep you posted.

Take care, Mom. Keep up your faith in the Lord. He's taking care of us in His own way.

Love,
John

March 10, 1977

Dear Mom and Dad,

I arrived in Kikwit from Kinshasa last Saturday and here in Idiofa from Kikwit on Tuesday. As far as I know, my physical was OK—all the doctor could find was a skin fungus, which I've had all along. The fungus forms a little white spot, like this "O" and is spread sparsely over my back, chest, and arms.

151

It's no big deal, isn't noticeable, and I can easily kill it with a sulfur cream when I leave the tropics.

I found another mite in my toe on Monday, though I never felt it because it was under my little toe instead of under a toenail (that hurts with the swelling of the insect). Since I never felt it, it was able to completely mature to a large pea-sized sac of eggs. I cut open the entire swelling with a razor blade, pulled out the sac of eggs, and cleaned out the equally deep crater in my toe with alcohol. The problem isn't the mite but the infection that could follow if the wound isn't kept clean. It has healed up OK.

While in Kinshasa I spoke to the P.C. ag/fish director (Greg Vaut, who took over Steve Anderson's job) about the Progrès Populaire fish station. It turned out that P.C. needs a training site for this year's P.C. fishery trainees. P.C. was originally going to have all P.C. Africa fishery training in Cameroon, where I had my training. But the Cameroon government needs the station for other purposes, so only P.C. Cameroon trainees can go there.

That left us with two choices. Either terminate the P.C. Zaire fisheries program or train new volunteers here. So I now have another job to do. In four-and-one-half months, I have to build seven ponds for the trainees as well as arrange housing, food, and all the other logistics necessary for a ten-week training session. I'm now making all the estimates for the construction, housing, etc., and will talk with Greg on the Kikwit radio next week for the final OK. Wish me luck if we go ahead with all this, I'll need it. I think I'm becoming like you, Dad, a little overextended.

This morning I transported fifty fingerlings to a pond forty-five miles south of here. A bush priest is working with the villagers there, and I hope that with his encouragement and supervision they'll be able to raise fish. It's a poor region down there, and they don't have much food of any quality, especially during the dry season when all the gardens dry up.

I carried the fish in a five-gallon jug placed in a rack on my motorcycle. They were in the jug for two hours and they had a bumpy ride, yet not one of them died.

Mom, I've received your Feb. 14 letter. I'm glad my letters are arriving again. I'm sorry to hear the flu has had its rounds; it is I who should worry about your health problems instead of the other way around. The shirts do get ironed, but it's a charcoal iron so it won't melt polyester anyway.

Love to all,
John

March 18, 1977

Dear Mom and Dad,

It looks like Zaire has gained international attention again. There's no telling what may happen either to the country or to us. I certainly pray that Zaire doesn't have another revolution on her hands. If that happens, then a lot of development work done in the last ten years will be wasted.

The problem is that this country is ripe for a revolution. The economy has hit rock bottom. Zaire has no money. They can no longer buy refined petroleum products, and gasoline is now scarce. I have ten more liters of fuel, and then that's it. The only thing keeping Kinshasa going is Shaba's copper. So I don't suppose it would be surprising if Shaba became upset with the government's bad management using up their wealth.

This country never has completely settled down from the early sixties. A large problem with Africa is that there is still a lot of intertribal hostility and competition. The president is from Equateur, so automatically people from Bas Zaire, Bandundu, Kasai, Shaba, and Kivu aren't content with the regime. In 1965, Idiofa was completely devastated by the government's forces because it was the center of a revolutionary movement. It would be a long time before, and I doubt if there will be, another armed uprising in Bandundu, but nevertheless the resentment is here.

That's enough of that. Let's hope everything works out calmly.

I have no new fishery news. I'm waiting for Greg Vaut's (the ag/fish P.C. director) reply to my training center estimates. It would cost around 2,000 zaires for food and lodging. I hope we will be able to continue the fishery program.

It turned out we can't use the diplomatic pouch, so you needn't send me any thirteen-cent stamps. Washington turned down P.C. Kinshasa's plan because it would be in competition with international mail. So, I'll continue to never know if my letters are making it or not. I believe mail has been fairly good, though.

Love,
John

April 4, 1977

Dear Mom and Dad,

I am sorry to hear of all the hardships that have arisen at home; yet I'm sure that all will work out. I'm sorry that I'm so far away that I can't lend a hand; my thoughts and prayers are with you, though. Dad, you need never worry about burdening me with troubles at home. Though I'm far away, you still are and always will be my family. I know you all will handle things quite well without me; yet if it were possible, I would have come home. We are a big family, and crises are bound to arise. There are a lot of bumps in life. We can only ask the Lord to show us the way and guide us through life's difficult moments.

Work in Idiofa is progressing. I think there are over sixty people working on their fish ponds. I have to now turn down people who ask my advice, for otherwise I would spread myself too thin.

The Shaba problem has only affected us in that there is no more gasoline in Idiofa. There never will be a military confrontation in Bandundu; the region is too poor, and no one is interested in it. However, if Zaire plunged into serious military and economic disasters, Peace Corps may well pull out. There is certainly no hint of this yet, and I pray it never happens. There's no way to provide a durable service if you keep moving around.

Love,
John

April 24, 1977

Dear Everybody,

I'm in Kinshasa again. It seems I'm passing through here more and more frequently. Peace Corps is having an African regional fisheries conference in Bangi, Central African Empire, and two other fish guys and I are going up there.

We arrived here last Wednesday from Kikwit, and since then I have prepared a fifteen-page project status report and a narrated slide show for the conference. We leave Kinshasa tomorrow morning for a three-day layover in Douala (short vacation on the Atlantic) and on to Bangi Thursday for eight days.

Two F.A.O. fisheries experts have been in Kinshasa doing research on lake and river fisheries in Zaire. We spent quite a bit of time with them and went to look at a fish culture research station (not much work being done there) and an industrial fish culture center that is under construction. One of them (the experts) is the world's foremost authority on Tilapia systematics, and so we gained quite a bit of useful information from him. One interesting tidbit we learned was that the fish we're raising isn't a pure stock of Tilapia nilotica but rather a stable hybrid of T. nilotica and T. mossambica. So we now know that we should selectively breed our fish to acquire a fish with proper nilotica traits.

We spent this afternoon on a beach along the Zaire River's rapids just downstream of town. There's an amazing amount of water flowing down the rapids that must be two miles wide. It's estimated that the Zaire River from Kinshasa down has fifty percent of the world's potential hydroelectric power. Once this place gets its government organized, it'll be the richest country in Africa. (Hence the problems in Shaba. Everyone wants a piece of the pie!)

Dear Susan,

How are you? I am feeling fine. Thank you for your letter of April 2. I am glad you are doing well in ballet. Too bad you got an "I" in spacing on your report card. Ask Bob to help you in spacing, and next time you will get an "S."

Sue, did you get the golden egg at the Easter party? We hunt for eggs all the time in Zaire just to eat. I now have five ducks so I will soon have plenty of duck eggs.

Bye Sue and everybody else,
John

May 7, 1977

Dear Everybody,

I'm back in Douala, Cameroon again after one week in Bangi, Central African Empire. We were supposed to have arrived in Kinshasa last night, but the airline made a mistake with our reservations. The airline (UTA) is paying our room and board at a Catholic mission until we leave tomorrow.

Our meeting in Bangi went very well. We gained a lot of good information learning how the Peace Corps fishery programs are run in other countries. P.C. has fisheries volunteers in Zaire, Cameroon, C.A.E., and Niger. (They didn't make it, though. They were grounded due to a sandstorm.) P.C. is planning fishery programs in Chad, Upper Volta, and Senegal, and there were representatives from each of these countries. U.S.A.I.D. sent a fisheries man from Washington to attend the meeting and see what P.C. is doing. They have funded a lot of P.C. fishery programs, and we may receive $70,000 a year for five years to support our program in Zaire.

Bangi is more like a small European town than an African city. We stayed in a modern hotel that was similar to a Holiday Inn. It had a beautiful outdoor terrace surrounded with trees and tropical plants and a fair-sized swimming pool where we spent our siesta hours.

The town is on the Oubangi River, and there was a beautiful beach just below the hotel. Last Sunday we played Frisbee (Jim's) all afternoon. A friend and I swam halfway across the river (maybe three-quarters of a mile round trip). It's the end of the dry season, so the water's very low and there wasn't much of a current.

The town is full of French-run bars and restaurants, so we ate very well. It was as if we were back in the States except that you spoke French with the waiters. I even ate two pizzas one night.

The ambassador invited the whole group over to his house one evening for beer and cheese. He and his wife were very hospitable. C.A.E. is small enough so that the Americans can form a fairly close community. There are too many Americans in Zaire and there is no community feeling.

We also toured an F.A.O. fish station and one volunteer's site. It was interesting to find out that our farmers are doing a more intensive culture than all the other countries are, and that our production figures are higher. I guess we're doing something right in Zaire.

Love to all,
John

May 14, 1977

Dear Mom,

I'm back in Idiofa after coming back from the fisheries conference. We arrived in Kinshasa Sunday the 8th, flew to Kikwit on Tuesday, and I rode to Idiofa in a Progrès Populaire truck Thursday. It's great being back on the job. Hopefully I won't leave Idiofa again until December.

There were a dozen letters waiting for me when I came back. Jim's pictures arrived, Alice Gravely has a baby boy, I heard from Debi, Mary Smart, Karen, Fr. Magee (surprise), Dad, Bob, Sue, and several letters from you (one dated April 4). If anyone is still worried or asks about the Shaba problems, there is no need to worry. We're seven hundred miles from the area, so you can consider us as being in another country.

For a while we thought that there would be no trainees coming, but when I arrived back in Kinshasa, I found out that there will be seven to nine new fish volunteers. So that gives me just two months to get things organized here. We have twenty workers building ponds at the station and hope to finish seven, 20 X 15 meter ponds by July 15. Plus, I have a lot of farmers waiting on me to bring them fish. So, I'm super busy.

Please send me the new addresses of the Godlewskis. I'd like to write and see how they're doing.

Boogie will have her pups in a week or two. Everyone wants a pup, so I know I'll gain a lot of enemies, for I can't give everyone a pup. She almost died while I was gone. I was told she became so weak that she couldn't keep her tongue in her mouth. The vet gave her a couple shots of penicillin and she pulled through OK. I hope the pups weren't affected.

We'll all be getting new motorcycles soon—Honda 125 trail bikes shipped in from the States. The ones we have are still OK, but they're street models and are a bit too small for the heavier guys.

Supposedly the airline service has started again to Idiofa. That would cut mailing time down to ten days if it's true. Some things seem to be getting better. We have gasoline and diesel fuel, but now there's no kerosene for the stoves and refrigerators.

Love to all,
John

May 27, 1977

Dear Mom and Dad,

Sounds like Jim and Tom are still carrying all the honors away. Pass on my congratulations. I've received mail in nine days; weekly air service has restarted from Kinshasa to Idiofa. Plus, I can use the diplomatic pouch to mail stuff (small!) home. I'll be able to use those thirteen-cent stamps Jim sent me now.

Boogie died this past Sunday. She was very sick two weeks ago while I was still gone. She recovered, but I think her pups died. She never aborted, so I suppose that caused her death. She was a good dog. Maybe I'll get another one, or perhaps a cat.

I've got more work than I know how to handle. I finally have a good quantity of fingerlings and am transporting them all around. Plus, more and more people ask me to come see their ponds. I still have a lot of work, too, for the seven to nine new fishery trainees who'll arrive July 20 or so.

We harvested one of the farmer ponds I was working on while I was in Kikwit that Doug took over. They had the best production we've ever seen and possibly the best for Peace Corps/Africa: two hundred kg (440 pounds) of fish after six months, from a pond twenty meters by twenty meters square. That's a lot of fish from one small pond.

Love to all,
John

June 8, 1977

Dear Dad,

Everything's going along fairly well here. The twenty workers for Progrès Populaire are finishing about three, twenty m by fifteen m ponds a month, so in a few months we'll have fresh fish all the time. I'm organizing food and lodging for nine new fishery trainees. It'll be nice having a couple more PCVs in the area to help me out. My extension program is another full-time job, too. Lately I've been stocking around one thousand fingerlings per week in various farmers' ponds. We both may be spreading ourselves too thin.

It's amazing how many things that we consider normal aren't everyday knowledge here. I spent two days teaching the workers how to push a wheelbarrow, and had a hard time explaining to a farmer that you have to give your chickens water during the dry season.

Could you please order a couple of subscriptions for me? I don't know if there's any more money in my account, so just keep the tab if there's no more money, and I'll reimburse it in December. There are two subscriptions I'd like you to order, please: *Commercial Fish Farmer and Aquaculture News* and *Mechanix Illustrated.*

Take care, and don't overwork
yourself,
John

June 16, 1977

Dear Mom and Dad,

We had a crisis at the fish station this week. The workers had not been doing a good job for several days, and we suspected some thievery for some time (catching and selling fish at night). Some fish died Saturday (poisoned?) so I checked on the ponds Sunday to see if more fish died. They didn't expect me to show up Sunday, so I caught four workers using station tools to dig their own ponds. It may sound cruel, but we fired those four (of twenty) workers, plus the sentry who let the tools out.

Development work is difficult and becomes almost impossible when the country's economy is shot. Whereas a $20 per month salary used to be a worthwhile wage three years ago, inflation has ruined everything. A common laborer cannot possibly support a family, so you can understand thievery. Yet at the same time, if you let little things slide by, they'll only grow, and we'll never have a functioning fish station. So, you have to be a nasty boss and fire a few before the whole bunch has to go.

On Tuesday I worked all day moving earth with the rest of the workers, and after work I played the preacher for about five minutes. I had to explain to them that the development of their country is in their hands and *petits vols* will only retard things all the longer. They thought that the fish station's purpose was so that the white man could earn more money. So I had to explain how the station is to help them and their people by providing an adequate supply of good fingerlings, by providing a good example on how to build and manage fish ponds, etc. The workers seemed to have taken my advice quite well, for yesterday and today they worked extra hard. It's strange being a teacher and a preacher to men twice my age.

I'm going into the duck business. I have one drake and six hens. They should start laying in July, so I hope to have all kinds of ducklings swimming in the ponds soon. You only need to feed them a little bit, for they find a lot of food in the ponds. I'll have to find out how many ducks a pond can support. When we're a little better organized, I'll start a rabbit project, too.

That's all the news for now. All's well and slowly coming along.

Peace to all,
John

June 29, 1977

Dear Little Sis Sue,

How are you? I am OK. Thank you for all your letters.

We are now in the dry season in Zaire. It will not rain again until late September. All the grass and flowers are drying up. What are you doing this summer? Are you learning how to swim better? Let me know if you dive off the diving board.

Love,
John

June 29, 1977

Dear Mom and Dad,

Mail is slow on this end now; two weeks and no news. Hopefully, there will be some mail on tomorrow's plane.

I'm busy organizing the housing and training facilities for the coming volunteers. We're to have nine new fishery volunteers, and of them three will stay in my region. It should be nice having more people to share the workload. Harry Rea, who was one of our trainers two years ago, will arrive in Idiofa next week to organize the last little things before training starts.

During training I'll assist Harry with the fishery work. I have to read up on all the literature I have. My village work will take two giant steps backwards during training because I'll be so tied up there. With the extra volunteers later, we'll be able to do far better work, so that'll make up for the time lost.

165

Next month the Progrès Populaire will hire their own fishery extension agent who will be my counterpart. The main emphasis of my work will then be to adequately train him to carry on fish culture when I leave. He'll have to manage the small fish station we're building as well as explain to villagers how to properly raise fish. If I can leave someone good behind me who'll continue on, I'll have accomplished something worthwhile.

Next month will be interesting being a trainer instead of a trainee. My own training wasn't that long ago, and I still feel rather uninformed in many areas. Yet I'll have to play the know-it-all junior to a bunch of freshmen.

The trainees will have a rough time, and I'm sure I'll have to be a counselor, too. They'll have to study fish culture, French, and Kikongo and become used to a strange environment all at the same time. Hopefully, we'll accomplish our goals and have an enjoyable experience at the same time.

Is the family planning any trips this summer? Be sure to find enough time to relax.

Take care,
John

P.S. Dad - Happy 52nd!

July 16, 1977

Dear Mom and Dad,

I hope all are fine at home and have found time to relax. Summer will be over soon. It's our winter here, and I have plenty of work to keep busy and stay warm.

Last week we had a fondu dinner at the hotel in Idiofa. The pots were a present, so the owner of the hotel invited us over to try them out. We had beef, goat, sheep, and a combination of lung, heart, liver, and kidney for meat (no cheese). Noll (the German mechanic who is also an excellent cook) prepared about seven sauces to dip the fried meat into. It was excellent.

Recently, I visited for the first time two American women who live twenty-five kilometers from here. They run an orphanage for around forty children. They are mostly on their own with some monetary support from some American Protestant missions. They've been there since 1948 except for four years (1965–1969) during the rebellion. They were barely evacuated when the rebels arrived, destroyed the buildings, took all the animals, and killed all but the few older children who escaped on their own.

I was with a British director of OxFam who was here just after the rebellion, and he told me what it was like. He has traveled to almost all of the disaster areas in the world, and he said it was no different from anywhere else. There was no food, and people were living skeletons here not ten years ago. And now with the fall of the economy, people can no longer afford to buy quality food, and there's little wild game to augment the people's diet.

The OxFam director was fairly well impressed with the fish project and is willing to provide Progrès Populaire a Land Rover for the fish station we're building and maybe even provide the funds necessary to build a training center. After two years, things are warming up for us. If I stay another two years, I could accomplish something durable for these people.

Harry Rea, the trainer for the eight new fishery trainees, arrived in Idiofa Wednesday. We are now busy with the final preparations of the house, the ponds, the food supply, etc.

The trainees arrive tonight in Kinshasa, next Thursday (21st) in Kikwit, and Friday in Idiofa. Though three months ago I doubted if a stage would be possible. We're going to do it. I pray all will go well.

This is the biggest job I've had in my life, and I have so many things to think of it's hard to keep things straight. I'm building the station, running an extension program, organizing housing and the food, trying to be the treasurer, and I'll be an assistant trainer. Needless to say, I'm overwhelmed and will be glad when the trainees become volunteers. I'll be ready for a vacation come December.

That's the news for now. Take care.

Love,
John

July 26, 1977

Dear Mom and Dad,

Everything has finally fallen into place in Idiofa, and the new trainees have arrived. Last week was quite busy, finishing the preparations for food and lodging. But along with the trainees, the program administrator arrived who will take care of all the details now. This means I can go back to my fish job. The trainees are having two weeks of intensive French before starting fishery training. In these two weeks, I have to ready the fish station for them: finishing ponds, stocking supplies, etc. My role in their fishery training will be minimal during the first half of training. Later on I'll help out with the technical seminars.

For me, this is a good time to have new blood pumped into the system. After two years, a person can start to become complacent and lose some of that original drive and commitment that brings a volunteer over in the first place. Listening to these guys talk and work so hard learning French is an excellent incentive for me to search harder to improve my work.

Of the eight trainees, four will be within two hundred km of my post. I also have two Zairian counterparts in the works with the Progrès Populaire. One of my counterparts would run the extension program outside of Idiofa, and the other would manage the fish station. My role would then change from an extension worker to an administrator-teacher. I'll have to organize all the volunteers and counterparts, decide how best to run the station, and give training sessions to local farmers. I can see how eighteen months more could be very fruitful.

The trainees are very quick to join into local social life. We were at the hotel last Saturday night and the orchestra was playing. They all joined in dancing, tried speaking French, and had a good time. For someone coming out of the States for the first time, all this could be traumatic. The next two months will be the hardest for the potential volunteer. The staff member also has to be a guidance counselor.

I have to go visit the trainees. I hope all are well and enjoying the summer back home.

Love,
John

P.S. Tom—happy summer, old man!

August 16, 1977

Dear Mom and Dad,

Quite a few letters and postcards have been coming in. Received your letter of Aug. 1 with the snapshot today. Please thank the little kids for their postcards; I'm glad everyone had a good time at the beach.

The training has settled into a pattern now, and I am back on my regular job. We had a fiasco last week when we found out that there weren't any fingerlings in the Progrès Populaire fish ponds, and we needed 4,000 for the trainees. A couple of guys drove 160 km to another volunteer's post and harvested a pond to acquire the needed amount of little fish. All's well now. Each trainee has stocked his own pond and is busy raising his fish.

We do have a big fish culture problem in Idiofa Zone because the water is very acidic (pH 4.0–5.5) and soft. This is not conducive at all to fish growth and reproduction. We believe that, because I didn't properly lime the ponds, reproduction was reduced to almost zero. This is serious for a farmer who can't afford to lime his pond. I'm not sure how to resolve this. Many of my farmers' fish are growing slowly and/or aren't reproducing.

The trainees are adapting quite well to Idiofa. We play volleyball, football, or Frisbee, and several local kids always join in. We've gone dancing quite often and have also enjoyed Sunday afternoons at the swimming hole.

This past Sunday, I attended an ordination for a Belgian frère and a Zairian frère, who are now pères. The rite was completely in Kikongo and was extremely interesting. There is much participation in the ceremony: singing, applauding, and dancing. After the ordination, a group of women danced around the new priests, threw flowers on them, sang, and waved scarves in the air. They even had a little musket they fired quite often.

Tonight, Val Mezinis, the fishery trainer I had two years ago in Cameroon, will arrive in Idiofa. He is now in charge of all the Peace Corps fishery-training programs in the world. I think he's based in Washington D.C. He's checking out our fishery program in Zaire as well as the new training program. I sure could use some of his professional advice on my water quality problems. He has almost finished his doctorate in fish culture from Auburn University. Most of the fishery people at Auburn are former P.C. fishery volunteers.

Mom, you needn't worry about the family growing up and moving out on its own—that's the way it's supposed to be. I'd be more worried about someone who couldn't move out and cope with the world.

Take care and love to all,
John

Note: During the volunteer training program I fell off my motorcycle and suffered a broken collarbone. Peace Corps flew me to the U.S. Army hospital in Frankfurt, Germany, for observation.

September 5, 1977

Dear Mom and Dad,

I'll leave Frankfurt tomorrow at 6:55 P.M. and arrive in Kinshasa the next morning. Seeing Frankfurt was nice, but it's a bad time to be off the job. I won't be able to drive a motorcycle for a while, but I can always walk. The fracture seems to be healing OK; I now have almost full mobility with my right arm. As long as I don't jolt my right shoulder or lift anything too heavy in my right arm, there's no pain. There will be a noticeable bump, however, in the middle of my collarbone.

I've walked quite a bit around town. If I spoke or read German, my visit would have been far more interesting. As it is, I saw quite a few things: the zoo, several parks, a cathedral, the main cemetery, a town hall, and many small shops and restaurants. Especially after being as used to the slightly chaotic systems in Zaire, it certainly is impressive to see such a neat, orderly city. When I finish with the Peace Corps, I hope to find someone and travel through some of Europe for a month or so.

It was nice hearing a few people's voices over the phone. Jerry sounded a bit older. Dad, I think you're working too hard; you sounded a bit tired for 5:45 in the afternoon. Mom, you sounded as if in good spirits. Please remain that way. I'm sorry if I sounded a little sleepy-eyed myself. I'm so accustomed to going to bed at 9:00–9:30, it's a chore staying up until 11:00.

The next three months will go by quickly, and I'll find myself flying another jet plane across the Atlantic. December is one of the hotter months in Zaire. I hope I readapt quickly enough to winter back home.

Love to all,
John

September 16, 1977

Dear Mom and Dad,

I'm back in Idiofa. I arrived Wednesday evening. Sally Tripple, the P.C. doctor, was traveling up country, so I had to wait in Kinshasa one week until she saw me. I had an x-ray taken, and it showed the bone was healing all right, so she gave me the OK to come back to my post.

Tuesday morning I found a ride with OxFam from Kinshasa to Kikwit by Land Rover. Their field director and I left at 5:00 P.M. and arrived at 1:10 A.M. Wednesday. That morning I was fortunate to find Munkoko, the director of Progrès

Populaire, in Kikwit. He was going back to Idiofa that afternoon, so I made the trip Kinshasa–Idiofa in only twenty-five hours. The bouncing didn't hurt my shoulder.

One of the trainees had to go home suddenly because his mother died of cancer. If all goes well, he'll be back in two weeks.

The trainees are all having problems with those mites that grow under the skin of your foot. In the two years I've been here, I've only had about six, but the trainees have been infested. One guy who had some open blisters had twenty mites start to dig in the sore. They have to be very careful and keep those wounds clean, or they will become infected. Between the trainees and local kids, there are a lot of people around the trainees' house, and since they always play football or Frisbee in bare feet, I suppose that's how they got the mites.

During the last two weeks of training, each trainee will give a seminar on various aspects of fish culture. I missed the construction seminar Wednesday, but attended the water chemistry seminar yesterday (that's the one I presented two years ago in Cameroon). Since I can't do much extension work, I'll be attending all the seminars and help fill in any holes.

I had a reproduction problem down at the ponds because I let the pH remain at 5.5, which stopped egg production. (I didn't realize that.) The trainees have been liming their ponds to a pH of 7–9, and there now are thousands of baby fish.

I believe I told you Progrès Populaire has provided me with a counterpart. He's now using my motorcycle and visiting farmers. As soon as I get my new Honda 125, we'll be able to do a lot of work.

I think I figured out what I'd like to do after next year. Graduate studies at Auburn U. interests me, and then maybe

I could do more fish culture work in Latin or South America with the Catholic Relief Service, World Neighbors, or some organization like that.

Congratulations, Dad, on your treasury job offer; I hope all works out for the best.

Love,
John

September 30, 1977

Dear Mom and Dad,

The fishery training is now over. Everyone leaves for Kikwit tomorrow. Every one of the trainers drained his pond this week and recorded the results of eight weeks of raising fish. Some of the guys did well, having fair growth rates and good reproduction (12,000 fry were produced). However, in a couple of ponds there was negative growth due to up to fifty percent of the fish missing. We're not sure where they all went but certainly predation, disease, stress, and poaching all took a toll.

My collarbone is progressing fine. This Wednesday will be the sixth week, so I'll be able to remove my brace for good. The spring exerciser I bought in Germany is very handy. By adjusting the number of springs, I can do various shoulder exercises without straining the healing bone. I should be back to normal by December.

It will be nice to have Idiofa come back to normal. Various problems that cropped up during the past ten weeks of training have discouraged me a little. Some of my management techniques weren't too good at the station, and reproduction was thrown off just before the training. Due to this we had a fingerling crisis when the training began. Sometime before July, a lot of fish were stolen from the ponds, and that hindered my program substantially. Things are picking up, though, with those 12,000 fry. Plus, several of my farmers are getting excellent fish growth and reproduction.

The area I'm working in isn't very conducive to fish culture due to its sandy soils and acidic waters. This is why some of my projects have been mediocre. But because I am getting good results in certain areas, I have to figure out why in certain soils fish culture works and why in other soils it doesn't, though the soils seem similar.

Last night we celebrated the end of the training. We invited around forty people to drinks and dinner at the Hotel Diakal. All the department heads of P.P. came, plus the bishop, plus a local government official. We had an excellent dinner: soup, grilled tilapia (fish) appetizer, grilled chicken, French fries, tomato salad, and fruit salad. Steve Anderson, who is now working on a manioc project, was there, too. We all sat around talking afterwards until midnight or so.

I'll be excited to come home for Christmas. I also hope to find time in January to go down to Auburn, Alabama for a couple of days and check on their graduate fishery program.

Mom and Dad, I hope your future plans work out for the best.

Love, your son,
John

October 8, 1977

Dear Mom and Dad,

This past Thursday I had my collarbone x-rayed for the six-week check-up, which the P.C. doctor asked me to have done in Idiofa. To me it looked good, new bone is forming all around the fracture and the splinters are barely visible. I seldom feel the break anymore, but my shoulder does crack and pop when I use my arm, more so than it used to.

Bob MacAllister, the temporary P.C.Z. director who called you last month, and Dr. Irene Tinker, the Action (a P.C. affiliate organization) associate director for programs, planning, and the budget, came out to Idiofa visiting volunteers. They also talked quite a bit with Progrès Populaire people about their organization. P.C. would like to put more volunteers with the P.P. in health, fisheries, and agriculture. It's good the P.C. and Action administrators come out of the big city (Kinshasa, Washington, etc.) to see firsthand what the volunteers' job situations are like.

This country is in rough economic straits again. Gasoline is almost not to be found, so my job is seriously hindered. I can ride my motorcycle again (a little more wisely) but things look serious with the gas crisis. We've acquired a bicycle for the new fish volunteer, Mike Fitzgerald, who'll work 130 kilometers south of Idiofa. Hopefully we'll find another bicycle for our use around Idiofa.

There's a new PCV in Idiofa, Mark Ensler, from Minnesota, who'll teach chemistry and biology at the high school. He'll have a fair-sized house across the football field from where I live, so instead of living in the P.P. guesthouse, I may move in with him.

Jean Wajda, the French accountant for P.P. has just returned from a two-month vacation. So last night we had a *bon retour* dinner at the hotel. I caught a few fish that we fried up as an appetizer. The main course was an antelope roast, the best I think I've ever had here. We also had mounds of French fries, an excellent onion, tomato, and lettuce salad, and a banana-pineapple fruit salad for dessert. Mark was amazed at having such a meal in Idiofa after we had a forty-cent lunch of manioc and boiled pork, which still had hunks of skin with bristly hairs sticking out. After two years, I'm still not used to seeing such a dichotomy where ninety percent of the people can't afford to buy meat. Yet this could be one of Africa's richest nations if it were properly organized.

No mail has arrived for ten days. I hope the Zaire postal service is still operating. Due to lack of fuel, Air Zaire has reduced its number of flights. Many new Peace Corps teachers have been marooned in Kinshasa and haven't been able to go to their posts.

I hope everyone's well at home.

Love,
John

October 13, 1977

Dear Dad,

I received your letter yesterday. Thanks for ordering those magazines. Hopefully, they'll arrive before my time in Zaire comes to an end.

Please keep track of all the money I owe you; it must be adding up to a healthy sum. An Action official carried another roll of film home. You should have received it a while ago. Thanks, too, for paying my U. of MD dues and for sending the driving permit form. I've mailed it directly to Glen Burnie.

Though you'll get this late, Happy 26th Anniversary. I enjoy thinking back one year ago while I was home. This year's celebration won't be as grand, I suppose. May you and Mom have many happy returns.

We had a sad incident in the Idiofa diocese. A young Dutch priest died from an appendix that burst. It was a very bizarre case because the symptoms were not at all those of appendicitis. He had slight abdominal pains for a week, but because it never was intense or localized, he thought it was malaria or maybe liver problems. But then it became a little worse, and a nurse at his mission diagnosed it as appendicitis. Nobody was yet alarmed, and he didn't leave to the hospital until the next day. After the six-hour drive, he was still feeling fairly well. He was always walking and even played cards that night. The next morning, Père Pete walked to his own surgery. But when the doctor operated, he found that the appendix had already burst and the infection was quite advanced. The doctor cleaned out the infection the best he could and closed the père, but the infection returned and his condition worsened. A few days later, they operated again and installed several drains, but the doctor only gave Père Pete two days to live.

Pete remained conscious and knowledgeable the whole time and was still living six days later. He even celebrated a mass from his bed. Because it was so strange the Père was still alive, the doctor decided to attempt a third operation only to find the intestines disintegrating. Père Pete died the following morning, which was yesterday.

The funeral services were yesterday evening. I was able to follow most of the Kikongo service and songs for about the first time. All the thoughts expressed by the people were quite moving. It's sad to see a young, energetic person go too soon. "Nzambi, ke binga bana na yondi na ntangu ya yondi" (God calls His children in His time).

C'est tout pour le moment, papa. I hope all your business ventures are going well.

Love,
John

November 2, 1977

Dear Mom,

We're into the rainy season in a big way now; it rains almost every day. It rained fairly hard yesterday afternoon, and there's a steady light rain now this morning. As soon as it slacks off I'll go out and visit a group of farmers in one village.

This past Monday we seined and sold over 4,000 fingerlings to an Idiofan merchant. He has built two one-third-acre ponds and is starting a fair-sized fish culture project. My counterpart is coming along fairly well in the job. He is well-motivated and quite interested in the work. I hope that he'll be able to continue on the project.

With Jerry, Bob, Sue, and yourself all playing something, the house must always have someone practicing their music. I may buy a cornet or a trumpet when I come home. I'd like to start playing again. Noll used to play a cornet, too, so that would give us something else to do.

Mike (new PCV English teacher) only lasted a week in Idiofa. He decided that there just weren't enough distractions around to occupy his free time. He's now in Kikwit and may teach there or may simply return home.

Mark Ensler's coming along OK. He enjoys the town, people, and his school. We've played volleyball quite a bit and hope to build a basketball court. I also intend to bring a few softballs and a bat when I return from vacation. We should move into the house provided by the school by the end of this week.

My ducks have laid and hatched eighteen ducklings; however, sixteen of them have died. The male duck has killed a few, and I'm not sure why the rest have died. The price of meat is becoming so expensive you almost have to raise your own. A chicken is now five z ($6), and a duck would be nine z. Mark and I will start raising chickens, too, when we move in.

In about five weeks, I'll start my trek home. I'd like to arrive before Sue's birthday but don't know for sure when I'll arrive. Last year I was a little overly anxious to return to Zaire, but this year I've been gone long enough that I truly want to visit everybody. A lot has gone on with the family during the past year and being a far-away observer isn't what I want, but I suppose for now that's the way it is.

Take care and see you soon,
John

P.S. I received a nice surprise at Noll's at breakfast. He had written "Happy Birthday to You" on a piece of paper and put a marigold in a vase.

November 10, 1977

Dear Mom and Dad,

This week Mark and I moved into our new house. It's huge for two people: three bedrooms, a bathroom, a living room-dining room complex, a storage room, and a kitchen. The interior has been recently painted and everything is in fair repair. We have electricity through the working day and in the evening, and we'll probably shortly install an electric refrigerator. There's running water, too, though we have a few leaks to fix.

The yard is another story, though. There's a bad erosion problem from the runoff from the high school. Hopefully we'll be able to divert that and plant grass on the bare areas. We'll fence in a garden area, too, and I'll start raising chickens again. It was in a way a shame, though, to leave the cozy, little room I had in the P.P. guesthouse.

Fish work is keeping me super busy. Yesterday I rode the bicycle forty km, checking out five pond sites. That wasn't too bad, but I'm tired out today, even though I drove the motorcycle. I spent two-and-one-half to three hours climbing up and down steep hills through jungle looking at new fish sites. Tomorrow and Friday will be the same thing. Saturday will be my most important fish harvest up to now, for it will show approximately what the maximum production in savanna soil fish ponds is. The results will be somewhat less than maximum, though, for the farmer has already netted and sold over 4,000 fingerlings.

I can't even take a break this Sunday, for I have another harvest at 6:00 A.M. and then I have to catch 2,500 fingerlings at the P.P. station. That afternoon I'll have to haul the fish to the village waiting for them and then continue on to the P.P. agriculture training center where I'll spend all next week finishing four ponds. During that time, I'll be using the bicycle, and at the end, I'll ride it the fifty-six km back to Idiofa.

Time's going by fast, as it always does. It'll be December before I know it with all this work I now have. My counterpart, Sala, is learning the job fairly well. I hope he'll be able to carry on OK while I'm home.

I won't know my ETA until I go to Kinshasa. I'll leave Idiofa around the 8th, be in Kinshasa around the 10th, and hopefully arrive home by the 16th or 17th. I'll stay for around four weeks. Peace Corps should be able to book me to National Airport.

Hope all's well at home, work, and school.

Love to all,
John

November 29, 1977

Dear Mom and Dad,

All's well here. On Dec. 10th I'll leave Idiofa and arrive in Kinshasa that afternoon. Since the paved road is completed from Kikwit to Kinshasa, we can do the whole trip in less than fourteen hours.

In the last two weeks I've only been in Idiofa for about four days; sorry I haven't written. This will be the last letter before I come home.

We're finally starting to get some positive results with a couple good harvests. A group of three farmers made over 300 z ($345) from a sixteen by twenty yard pond in six months. This is amazing, considering that under traditional fish culture practices, they only made 30 z in one year.

Another farmer made 60 z in four months from a twenty by ten yard pond. This is excellent in itself, but we only stocked thirty-seven small fingerlings in a pond where we

should have stocked two hundred fingerlings. I'm sure he could have more than doubled his production. The Progrès Populaire fish station is starting to make money, too. We have thousands of fingerlings, and I hope to sell four to five thousand per month. Yesterday we netted two thousand and will haul fourteen hundred to Mike Fitzgerald, the new volunteer working at Ngashi, a mission 140 km south of Idiofa.

My counterpart is doing well. If the Progrès Populaire continues to support the fisheries project, I'm sure he'll do a good job.

The P.P. is running into some problems now. This year they commercialized 1,300 tons of rice, and, instead of primarily concerning themselves with the small village farmer, a lot of the P.P. administration is focusing on rice marketing. They used to have extension teams who would regularly visit farmers and advise them on crop production, cattle production, etc. However, the fish program is now the only team that continues to see villagers. Tribal jealousies are coming into play, too. It's a long, complicated story and African development has a long way to go.

It stems from the fact that it is traditionally wrong for anyone to break the status quo. My best fish farmer is considered a fool in his village because he works so hard. His wife was even taken away from him because he wasn't considered normal. Two weeks ago when we harvested his first pond, he had fished out almost all of the fish before we drained the pond because he didn't want anyone to see how well he did or how much money he made. His ponds, or even he, could be poisoned because he's doing so much better than everyone else. Once, in this village, a farmer was doing an excellent job raising pigs. But then one night someone came in and killed all thirty animals.

It's frustrating for me to see how badly these people need protein in their diets, and I know fish culture can help them. But when villagers have their initiative suppressed by their elders, I wonder what their future is.

See you soon,
John

Clockwise from the top: Bill's house, a savanna house (no clay), Mike's house, Art's house, Kabuya (the director of the Laba agriculture center) and his family

186

Clockwise from top: A motorized ferry crossing, Doug and a
village woman cooking, women coming home from the fields,
dinner; luku (manioc dough ball), saka-saka (manioc leaves), and
nsusu moimba (chicken in palm oil sauce), a forest trail

187

Chapter Six

Idiofa, Zaire
1978

January 29, 1978

Dear everybody,

I've had a good trip so far heading back to Idiofa. Today I'll leave Kikwit with Dr. Sally Tripple and the P.C. regional representative (Nelson Sorbo) on a short trip before arriving in Idiofa Tuesday.

Dennis Murnyak, another Zaire fish PCV, flew back to Zaire on the same Pan Am flight. He has changed programs and now is in wildlife researching gorillas.

I spent two days in Kinshasa and found a quick ride back to Kikwit. OxFam asked me to drive one of their Land Rovers with a new Honda 125 motorcycle to Kikwit for them. I did that yesterday and fortunately had no mechanical troubles. It's nice seeing everyone in Kikwit again; Steve Anderson says hello.

Steve is working for the International Institute of Agriculture organizing a manioc project for Bandundu region here. There has been no selective breeding work done with manioc, and, in certain areas, the plants are starting to degenerate and become more prone to diseases. So Steve looks for hardy plants, takes cuttings from them, plants the cuttings in experimental plots, and then redistributes the improved variety. Since manioc is the staple carbohydrate, any improvement in the plants' performance is important.

Dr. Sally has been in Bandundu for about one week visiting all the PCVs. She enjoyed being home for Christmas. Her parents didn't know she was coming. She arrived Christmas Eve; her brother snuck her into the house, and then they tied a ribbon and bow around her and presented her to her mom. I bet that was fun.

Zaire is going through some very rough times. I don't know if any news is coming to the States, but the political situation is not good. There have been open manifestations against the government and the military has retaliated. That's all I should say for now.

We'll be leaving shortly for Due, Mbeo, Ngosso, and finally Idiofa. I hope everyone is still well. I love you all.

Take care,
John

February 19, 1978

Dear Mom and Dad,

I received your first letter from Jan. 31. Things in Idiofa have quieted down; most of the army has left. They took most of the goats, chickens, and sheep from the surrounding villages. The villagers don't have much left to eat. Kwashiorkor is serious enough and will now only get worse. Our petition to President Mobutu denouncing the commissaire de zone should have been presented this past week. The outcome of this will more than likely be zero. But we hope the present commissaire will be removed from office.

We've been playing quite a bit with the local kids. Two PCVs spent their semester break with Mark and me, and they taught the kids quite a few songs in English. I accompanied them on harmonica. We have a couple of good Frisbee throwers, too. The water rocket I brought back was an instant success, and recently we've added water pistols to our toy box.

As I said, Idiofa is returning to normal but until we hear some kind of a reply to our petition it will remain a wait-and-see situation. A lot of poor people in the world are suppressed; if we are to help them we can't let their governments discourage us. Yet the U.S. government has provided a lot of economic and military assistance to Zaire. I wonder what the future holds—will the U.S. continue to support this regime, or what?

Love,
John

February 26, 1978

Dear Mom and Dad,

Received your February 8 letter with Sue's Valentine's Day card. Tell her I love her, too.

I've heard Kinshasa is having its problems again. Many people are disenchanted with President Mobutu, and they're becoming more and more vocal. I, too, am faced with a lot of frustrations. I've wanted to help the Zairian villager, but since there is no support whatsoever coming from this government, I know my project won't get off the ground. If the state cannot help their own people develop themselves, there is little a foreigner can do.

Give my best to the Dixons. I hope Mr. Dixon and Danny are improving.

The weather has been hot and dry. Not much rain has fallen for the past two months. The people have just planted their millet crop; hopefully it won't burn up. Hope your weather has started to warm up again. You're a courageous woman, Mom, to drive the family all over town all the time.

Hope all are well,
John

March 8, 1978

Dear Dad,

I've received Mom's Feb. 14 and Jim's Feb. 17 letters, it seems mail's coming through to me all right. I have my doubts, though, that mail is getting out of this country regularly.

There are more problems in this country. The president of Zaire has purged the army of some 250 officers from Kasai and Shaba regions. Many of these men are believed to have been killed. How much longer Mobutu can carry on like this I don't know. I've written President Carter and Ambassador Cutler (Zaire) asking why the news of all the abridgment of human rights in Zaire hasn't been broadcast for so long to the American public. Of course my voice from the wilderness won't amount to much. The United States has supported this corrupt, repressive regime of Mobutu for years, and I hope that now that Mobutu has proven himself to be nothing more than a murderer, U.S. support for his regime will cease.

It is depressing for me to come to a "developing" country to try and help a people help themselves, while the state does its best to suppress its people's development and now has even resorted to killing many common people.

I'm learning it's a complicated world, Dad, with no simple answers. I will continue to help what few people I can while I'm here, but will have to do some serious thinking when I come home to decide how to steer the rest of my life.

Love, your son,
John

March 20, 1978

Dear Mom and Dad,

I just received your March 7 letter, and it's obvious my letters aren't coming home. I mailed letters Jan. 30, Feb. 2, 8, 13, 19, 26, Mar. 8, and today. Now I intend to mail all my letters via someone returning to the States if possible.

I'm doing fine. Just today my new Honda 125 motorcycle arrived in Idiofa. Tomorrow I'll assemble it and give her a test spin. My old Yamaha has gone 20,000 miles over some terribly bad, dirt roads. She has never left me stranded, so I can't complain.

We had an excellent fish harvest at the P.P. agriculture center at Laba (Jim was there in January). They harvested fifty kg of fish from a two-hundred-square-meter pond only three months after stocking. In clay soil, fish culture is great. Most of my ponds are in sandy soil, but even there, fish culture is worthwhile, though you only have one-fifth of the production.

You asked me a lot of questions, Mom, so I'll answer them.

Since the troubles in Idiofa began, the kids haven't been flying their kites. Unfortunately, I broke both of mine. I intend to fix them and entertain the town again soon.

Eating is never a problem. Yesterday, we gave a duck dinner for eight, and that evening we were invited to a rabbit dinner. That, of course, isn't standard fare; usually we have canned or dried fish, rice, and beans. Village meals are always the most interesting; lots of strange dishes.

Bob McAllister is no longer with P.C. Zaire. He was only an acting director and has now returned to the D.C. area.

Congratulate Rose and Bob for me. I'm glad they're doing well in basketball. I'll be able to watch them play next year.

Say hello to the Dixons for me; I hope Danny and Mr. Dixon are both progressing well. I'm sorry about the mail problems, I know you've been worried. But October will come too soon as it is, so all will work out.

Love to all,
John

April 12, 1978

Dear Mom and Dad,

It's good to hear that some of my mail has made it home. You're right, Dad, in that it wasn't very wise to mention all that was happening in Idiofa. Not so much because my actions could have endangered me, but because I probably needlessly worried you. It seemed to me that all the abridgments of human rights in Zaire were not being exposed to the American public, so I had to tell my part. I wrote President Carter and

195

the U.S. ambassador to Zaire asking what the U.S.'s position on all these problems is.

Please keep that marine biology brochure at home. I'll check into it this fall.

I've had a few good harvests lately. My most progressive farmer has one, one-half-acre pond and has almost completed a three-quarter-acre pond. He harvested 340 kg of fish from his first pond last week. Fish culture is an excellent means of animal production here as well as a profitable business. It's the continuation of the job that will be difficult. I have a Zairian counterpart to whom I'm teaching the trade. But with the political problems, we may get no funding and the whole project could fall through.

Another problem has arisen in my most successful village. The chief wants each fish farmer to give him a goat, or else they can no longer raise fish. I don't know where this one will end, but it's something else we have to deal with.

This is a typical example of the greatest obstacle to Zairian, and even African development. Many people with any power are only interested in their own gain and very jealous if anyone else improves himself. Thus, the chiefs clamp down on any progressive individual. In some villages, farmers may have to pay the chief twenty-five percent of their grain production. I've even heard of pig projects and fish ponds being poisoned. This discourages the common man so much he no longer tries harder, and only works enough to exist.

Zaire faces a natural disaster in Bas Zaire (the region south and west of Kinshasa). They are having a serious drought, and the crops are about burnt up. This region is normally the breadbasket of Kinshasa, so this drought, combined with a decrease of imports (Zaire never pays its foreign debt), spells serious famine for the capital.

I hate giving such depressing news all the time, but that's what's going on here. I am productive, though, and manage to keep my spirits up. I always pray that things will improve more rapidly for Zaire; hopefully they will, someday.

Love,
John

April 20, 1978

Dear Mom,

That was quite a bit of news I received last Sunday. I'm sorry I won't be home for the birth. [Nine years after sibling number ten was born, my mother was expecting sibling number eleven.] Take good care of yourself, and I'm sure all will be all right. A new brother or sister will be something to look forward to when I come home. My prayers are with you and *bon courage.*

Michael Fitzgerald, a new fish PCV south of Idiofa, was driving up to town last Friday when he drove his new Honda off a bridge. He fell ten feet into six feet of water. Fortunately he wasn't hurt, but the bike was underwater for two hours. He rounded up about twenty villagers, tied a cable onto the bike and pulled it out. A nearby Belgian missionary drove Mike and the bike up to Idiofa where we disassembled the engine, flushed it out, and rebuilt it. For a while, Fitz thought he had ruined his month-old motorcycle. But we have it running like new.

Love,
John

Clockwise from top: water rocket fun, Idiofa boy, new Honda 125s, hand-tilled millet field, fish-farmer training school, ripe millet crop, PCVs playing with Idiofa children

April 27, 1978

Dear Mom and Dad,

Hope all is progressing well at home. With the birth just six months away, I suppose things are starting to show. My prayers are always with you.

I wonder if mail is leaving Zaire. By your letters, it seems few are coming through. Outside of the family, I'm writing few letters now, since they'd probably be lost anyway.

Tomorrow I'm heading out on a one-week trip north to Ipamu, Mangai, and Dibaya-Lubue. They're about eighty miles away, so I can't expect to do much work there. But at least I'll have a few of those farmers come to Idiofa to see some decent fish ponds. Maybe they'll be able to go home and apply some of what they see.

In two weeks we're giving a farmer training session. Twenty-five village farmers from about fifteen villages will come to where we have our best ponds built, and for three days we will discuss various aspects of fish culture. This should give many people a lot of good ideas.

Sue, Bob, Rose, Jerry, Paul, Ann, Tom, Jim; I miss you all. Be good and help one another.

Love,
John

199

May 16, 1978

Dear Mom and Dad and everybody,

Zaire's in turmoil again, sooner or later it'll fall. It's a wait-and-see situation right now. There are no problems in our area, but the military is tense.

We had a four-day farmer training session last week at Intswem, seven km from Idiofa. It went over very well. The farmers returned to their villages encouraged, with a better idea of what fish farming is all about. We also covered a lot of social and political problems farmers face raising fish. For once, they were able to exercise a freedom of speech that they don't normally have. People joining together to discuss common problems is rare in Zaire.

As I've mentioned before, it's a discouraging shame that every time a little progress is being made, something happens which strips away the few steps that you have made. I know a village farmer can improve his standard of living even in the poorest, sandy soil one finds. I pray that even if things fall apart now, that someday, someone will be able to use the knowledge that we've gained and carry on helping the villagers.

Hope everyone is well, and I'll say a special prayer for you, Mom.

Love,
John

May 31, 1978

Dear Mom and Dad and family,

Your letters are still coming in regularly, taking two to three weeks in transit. That's good news that my letters are coming through again.

Last week I flew to Kananga and drove to Mbuji-Mai and Gandijika. A.I.D., Peace Corps, and the Zaire government are planning to expand the fish program into the Kasai region. I accompanied an American and a Zairian engineer to do a cost estimate on reconstructing a fish station. It was an enjoyable trip. I saw a lot of Zaire and had a great flight in a Beechcraft light twin. But I took it with a grain of salt, for the Zairian government has never supported the work we are doing in Bandundu; now, with the Shaba problems, I doubt if this Kasai expansion will get off the ground.

Zaire is certainly beautiful, and, if properly organized, it could be almost a paradise. During the Kasai trip we lunched at a clear, blue lake that was two miles long and a mile wide. I enjoyed swimming in the warm water, encircled by rolling, grassy hills.

Your 4,700-mile trip sounds exciting. [My parents and siblings went on a long, cross-country vacation visiting many family members in Missouri, Texas, and Nebraska.] Say hello to all the family for me. You may receive this letter before you leave.

Diane Jennings has probably called you by today. She's a fine person. We were sorry to see her leave Zaire so soon. We've had several enjoyable times in Idiofa and Ngoso.

My prayers are with you,
John

June 26, 1978

Dear Dad,

Happy 53rd come the 13th. By now I suppose you've left on vacation and by the time you receive this you'll be home again. I hope all of the family was healthy while on vacation. I hope to be out for the harvest next summer, if I'm not back in school by that time. Your parents and brothers have always interested me; too bad I didn't know my grandparents better.

The Shaba incident never affected us directly. [The Shaba incident was one of several military actions where Zaire's army was involved.] It never will either because the Bandundu region has no riches to fight over. The American press is very quick to point its finger at the Cubans, who, I'm sure, are present, but they aren't the major problem. The problem is a tribal affair. The Katangese rebels and the Shaba people are from the same tribe. The rebels did not want to massacre anyone; things got out of hand when the Zairian military arrived on the scene. It isn't very prudent to always mention these things, so I guess that's enough. You can expect Zaire to smolder for quite some time, though.

Fish-business-wise, I keep good and busy. I'll be spending the better part of my remaining time at Laba, a Progrès Populaire ag. training center fifty-six km north of Idiofa. The production in our sandy soil ponds in Idiofa just isn't enough to make any money. So we have to build an acre's worth of ponds in the clay soil at Laba. They already have four small ponds that have had good production, so I'm fairly sure we'll be able to realize a fair profit.

Peace Corps is having a difficult time finding trainees to come to Zaire. The fishery program will suffer quite a bit. We originally wanted thirty new fishery volunteers this year, but Washington has only found three people willing to come to Zaire. It still hurts me inside to see the need these people have and to know that our program could do a lot more good. But, we all have growing pains, and this country is having a difficult childhood.

Mark Enzler (my housemate) had some interesting news the other day. His father is engaged again to someone with seven children (Mark's mom died in 1971 due to cancer). There are seven kids in Mark's present family so he'll be going home to a big family.

You, Mom, and the new child are all in my prayers. Hope all is progressing well.

Love, your son,
John

Clockwise from top: removing a fallen tree, Tilapia nilotica, pouring a concrete monk, new ponds at Laba agricultural center, building a pond dike

July 26, 1978

Dear Mom and Dad,

I've received several cards and letters; the latest letter is dated July 12. I'm glad you had a safe, enjoyable trip and hope Sue's infections have healed well.

I'm in Kinshasa working at the national fair. We have set up a display on the Peace Corps fishery program. The fair runs from the 15th until the 30th. Our job is to answer the questions of any inquisitive visitor. It's nice to see well-fed, nicely clothed children for a change. Most of the people at the fair are well-to-do Zairians.

Though my completion of service date is October 15th, I may stay on a little longer. We will have about twelve new volunteers for the fish program, and I'd like to see them to their posts. That would mean that I'd arrive home in January-February. As soon as I know for sure, I'll let you know.

At the fair, there is a display by the Zairian shipping company. I asked the representative about working on the ship to earn passage, but he said that there are so many people looking for work that it's almost impossible to do that. I would like to travel to Europe by boat, but I suppose I'll have to pay the ticket.

Mark Enzler and I had dinner last night with Ted Bratrud. Ted's doing a series of tapes interviewing people who were in Shaba during the recent war. He asked Mark and me to recount some of the events that occurred in Idiofa in January and February. Ted mentioned that a secret team of Zairians went into the Idiofa area after the problems to estimate the number of people killed. We always thought that from 500 to

1,000 people were killed, but Ted said the estimate is closer to 3,000. At any rate, I do wonder about President Carter's human rights campaign when these facts aren't told to the American people. More people were probably massacred in Idiofa than in Kolwezi.

Hopefully, I'll leave Kinshasa this Tuesday, Aug. 1. I'm anxious to get back to Laba and see how the pond construction is progressing.

Love,
John

August 8, 1978

Dear Mom and Dad,

I was saddened upon hearing about Ken and Rex's accident. [My cousin, Ken, was killed and his brother-in-law, Rex, was injured in a motorcycle accident in Nebraska.]

The telephone wasn't working in Kinshasa, so I wasn't able to call home. I did write Myrl, Walt, and family. The Lord has been kind to me during my motorcycle excursions. I pray that by remaining alert, and with Him watching over us, we'll remain safe drivers.

Work's coming along OK. My last few months are busy training my counterpart and building ponds at Laba. It's most likely now that my COS (completion of service) will be in mid-October. There is a chance that I'll work on fishery training in Oklahoma for a few months upon returning. It's a paying job, and I could use the money and experience.

In Kinshasa, I checked on returning by boat. It would be hard to work passage due to the high Zairian unemployment rate. It would cost me 900 z to go to Europe by boat.

Love,
John

Note: Unexpectedly, in early September 1978, I was asked to report to Norman, Oklahoma to participate in the training of the new Peace Corps Fishery Volunteers for Zaire. I arrived in Maryland in time to see my newborn baby brother for a few days. After completing the nine-week training program at Oklahoma University, I accompanied the trainees to Bukavu, Zaire, to assist in language, cross-cultural, and technical training.

Bukavu and Idiofa 1978-79

Chapter Seven

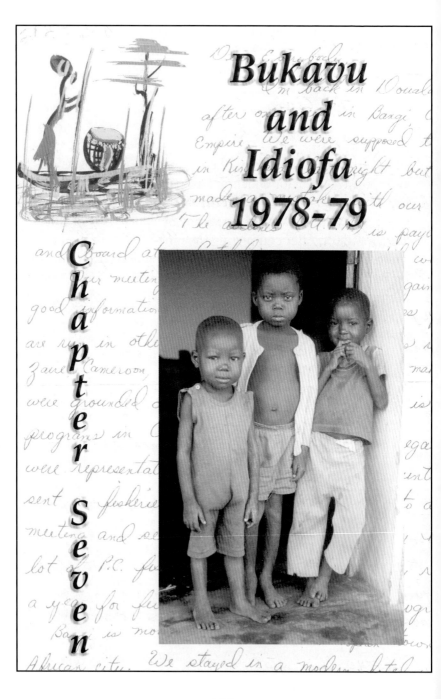

December 26, 1978

Dear Mom,

On the eve of your birthday, let me wish you a happy 49th. You're an amazing person for having given so much of yourself for so long, and still having an ample supply for the years yet to come. Few can accomplish what you have. We're all proud of you.

We had an enjoyable Christmas, though nothing seemed very Christmasy about it. Saturday night, we had a party inviting all of the teachers, their families, and the local PCVs. A few people danced until 4:00, though I only lasted until 2:00. The next night, Joe Hansen, the P.C. regional representative for Kivu, had a party at his house with more or less the same people. We ushered in Noël sitting on his cool, wind-swept balcony overlooking Lake Kivu. Christmas Day, a couple other trainees and I went to 10:30 mass. The singing sounded nice, but I can't understand Swahili. Those who went to midnight services said it was much better.

Christmas Day, I walked to Diane Jennings's house six kilometers from the center. She used to be stationed at Ngoso Mission fifty-six kilometers from Idiofa, where Mark Enzler and I rode to visit last Easter. Since she has had knee troubles, she has moved out here. She has a small house situated halfway up a steep hillside again overlooking the lake and the Rwanda Mountains. We had an American dinner of baked chicken, au gratin potatoes, and a tomato salad. The visit was a quiet break from the training center. She placed a small fir tree in her house, so I decorated it with one of the straw ornaments you gave me.

People here are quite different from those in Bandundu. No matter where you walk there, everyone will say hello to you. But here, they'll only give you a furtive glance and pass you by unless you say hello first. Nutritionally, they seem to

209

me far better off than back west. The soil is rich with beans and corn growing all the way up the steepest embankments. Dennis Murnyak, who trained in Cameroon with us and switched to wildlife studying gorillas his third and fourth years, speaks Swahili. Yet even so, they still aren't that open even to him. It may have something to do with the way the colonialists acted. Even today, only the upper class Zairians are expected to socialize with the whites, and whites rarely mix with villagers. Life would be less enjoyable here than in Bandundu, though the climate and scenery are beautiful.

I haven't heard from home yet but expect to soon. Hopefully my letters will make it OK through Rwanda.

Love and peace in the New Year,
John

Bukavu, Zaire
January 23, 1979

Dear Mom and Dad,

A PCV is coming home, so I'm taking advantage of her trip to send this. We only have two and one-half weeks of training left; things are busy but still progressing smoothly. One trainee has to go to Washington because of medical problems. It's a good excuse for her not to come back, for she really doesn't want to be a fish PCV, anyway. All of the other trainees are doing extremely well. They'll be good volunteers.

Clockwise from top: Mountain in Kivu Province, motorcycle training, Bukavu boy and scooter, Kivu countryside, surveying training, end of mountain top trek

The trainees had a taste of being on their own all last week. They visited several villages in rural Kivu, working in groups of two or three people with students from a rural development training school. They had to speak French, work with the villagers, and live and eat more or less as village people do. They came back bubbling with enthusiasm, content to leave the day-to-day, dull, repetitive language classes behind for a while. Actually, the exercise was excellent in improving their French because they couldn't resort to English. They also learned a lot about several development projects: spring improvement, cooperative development, garden planting, soybean planting, raising rabbits, etc. I wish I had a similar exercise three years ago; we would have been better volunteers for it.

On my way home, I hope to pass through Senegal and visit the Peace Corps fishery project there. Roger Palm, one of my training buddies, may be working there. After that, I intend to pass through England and visit Bob Gibsons' (Ox-Fam-Kikwit) mother. She visited us the same time Jim, Les, and Mary came over.

No letters have arrived for two weeks, but I'm sure everyone is healthy.

Love,
John

Idiofa, Zaire
February 19, 1979

Dear Mom and Dad,

After four and one-half months, the trainees have finally become P.C. Volunteers. Though the last few weeks did drag on, the group as a whole maintained their motivation and did an excellent job learning the basics of French and Kikongo. We lost two trainees; one became sick with mononucleosis and was sent home, the other just couldn't adapt to life in Zaire and decided to go home. The trainees

213

worked very diligently during their training and should become excellent volunteers.

I'm now back in Idiofa—arrived two evenings ago. We left Bukavu the 10th, spent four days in Kinshasa for a fishery meeting, and left Thursday for Kikwit. I then tuned my old motorcycle and drove to Idiofa Saturday.

Here's a quick rundown of my proposed itinerary:

Until Feb. 28	Idiofa
By March 5	Kinshasa
March 5–15	travel to Senegal and England, U.S.A., home
March 24	Oklahoma

Doc Clemens was in Kinshasa while we passed through. He is doing some programming work for Peace Corps, touring Tanzania, Kenya, Zaire, and Cameroon. It was interesting seeing him on our turf; he had many observations about our extension work in the Kikwit area. It's too bad Peace Corps can't have experts like him in the field more often to evaluate a country's fishery program.

We have to build thirty-two training ponds at the University of OK, so Doc asked me to be back as early as possible, preferably by March 18. I told him I needed some traveling time and time at home. I don't think they need me all that badly between March 1 and 24.

Training in OK will consist of two nine-week periods ending during late August. Having spent so little time at home the past four years, I intend to take the fall off before returning to OK for a master's of zoology program starting in January 1980.

Idiofa's the same. Mark and Francis still have the same daily routine they had six months ago. There is a new PCV in the house, Jennifer Hoyle, an English teacher from California. She seems to enjoy life here, as do the others.

I hope Matt and all the family are well. It will be great to come and see everyone again in a few weeks.

Love,
John

Epilogue

The United States Peace Corps maintained development programs in Zaire, Africa from 1970 until September 1991 when severe civil unrest forced the evacuation of all Peace Corps Volunteers. The inland fishery extension project grew from a single volunteer in 1974, to the eight of us described in this book, to sixty-five volunteers in 1989. During that year, the volunteers assisted over 1,500 fish farmers and helped them produce 100 tons of Tilapia nilotica (Peace Corps Congressional Presentation—Fiscal Year 1990). Over the course of seventeen years, Peace Corps Fishery Volunteers aided over 15,000 village farmers and trained numerous Zairian counterparts who could continue the work of training their own people. This program became the largest inland fishery program of its kind in the world. In 1984, a United States Agency for International Development evaluation team member described the program as the best of its type in Africa (*Peace Corps Africa Region Briefing Book*, 1985).

In closing, I would like to ask, why is it that we Americans are so willing to be so generous with people who are strangers and who are unable to help us in return? After both world wars, we spent billions of dollars without being reimbursed to help rebuild not only the nations of our allies but also those of our enemies. Every year, thousands of Americans join the ranks of the Peace Corps and other volunteer or mission organizations for little remuneration, and often at the cost of building a career. In recent war pictures, we have seen the same soldiers who in fierce combat one moment are yet moments later, risking their own well being to help a wounded enemy civilian or soldier off the battlefield to receive medical attention. Why do we so willingly engage in these benevolent gestures?

I believe the answer is found over and over again in the immutable benchmark of God's Holy Scripture. In the gospel of Luke, one finds the story of the Good Samaritan. In the book of Proverbs, we are told that he who gives to the poor will never want. In the gospel of Matthew, we are admonished to love our enemies and to do good to them that hate us, and pray for them.

It has been noted that the French philosopher and states-man Alexis de Tocqueville remarked in the 1830s that America is great because America is good, and that if America ceases to be good, she will cease to be great. Let us therefore be wise as a nation in this century and do good where and when we can. In that way we will continue to have the opportunity to share with the less fortunate God's blessings of human, material, and spiritual resources.

John Jochum
Summer 2004

Appendix

French Expressions

à bientôt	See you soon
agronome	government agriculture agent
assez régulièrement	quite regular
Bonne Année	Happy New Year
bonne arrivée	welcome (good arrival)
bonne chance	good luck
bonnes vacances	good vacation
bon retour	good return
Ce n'est pas bon, c'est mal.	That's not good, it's bad.
C'est tout pour le moment.	That's all for now.
Commissaire de Zone	Zone Commissioner
coup-coup	a grass cutting tool
domestique	house worker

219

en Afrique	in Africa
en brousse	in the brush (country)
enfin	finally
frère	brother
J'espère que tout le	I hope everyone
monde aura	will have
un bon été.	a good summer.
les enfants	the children
mal	bad, poorly
malheursement	unfortunately
marché	market
meilleurs voeux	best wishes
mon frère	my brother
mes frères	my brothers
patron	boss
Père Supérieur	Father Superior
petit vol	petty larceny
pourquoi	why
Qu'est-ce qu'il	What will happen?
y aura?	
Région	Region (political)
restez bien	stay well
sentinel	sentry
soeur	sister
Sous-Région	'Under' Region (political)
stage	training program
stagiaire	trainee
tour du monde	around the world
tout le monde	everybody
ville basse	lower town
Voix de France	Voice of France (short wave radio)
vulgarization	extension education

Kikongo Expressions

bwala	village
luku	boiled manioc flour
lupangu	fence, enclosure
mondele	a European (Caucasian)
nsusu moimba	chicken cooked in palm oil
pyote	small, round shelter made with palm fronds
saka saka	boiled manioc leaves

Abbreviations

A.I.D.	Agency of International Development
BBC	British Broadcasting Company
ETA	estimated time of arrival
F.A.O.	Food and Agricultural Organization (of the United Nations)
Fr.	Father
Kin.	Kinshasa, Zaire
L.R.	Land Rover (British vehicle)
OxFam	private, British foreign aid organization

P.C.	United States Peace Corps
PCT	Peace Corps Trainee
PCV	Peace Corps Volunteer
P.C.Z.	Peace Corps Zaire
PP	Progrès Populaire
PR	public relations
s.a.	such as
U. of MD.	University of Maryland at College Park
UTA	Union Transportation Aérienne (French airline)
VOA	Voice of America (short wave radio)
W.	west

Weights, Measures, and Currency

kilo	kilogram(s) (1 kg = 2.2 lbs.)
kg	kilogram(s)
lbs	pounds
gal	gallon
liter	approx. 1 quart
mpg	miles per gallon
km	kilometer(s) (1 km = 0.6 miles)
m	meter(s)
acre	43,560 square feet
are	100 square meters
hectare	10,000 square meters

z	zaire (currency)
k	makuta
	(100 makuta = 1 zaire)

To order additional copies of

LETTERS
FROMZAIRE

Have your credit card ready and call

Toll free: (877) 421-READ (7323)

or send $21.95* each plus $5.95 S&H** to

WinePress Publishing
PO Box 428
Enumclaw, WA 98022

or order online at: www.winepressbooks.com

*Washington residents, add 8.4% sales tax

**add $1.50 S&H for each additional book ordered